PEARSON RESOURCES

FOR INSTRUCTORS

DIAGNOSTIC and EDITING
TESTS and EXERCISES

to accompany

2011 Pearson English Handbooks
Thirteenth Edition

Revised by

Trudy Zimmerman
Hutchinson Community College

Joseph Little
Niagara University

Prepared by

David Anderson | John Feaster | Casey Gilson | Sally Harrold | Lucille Kish
Eric Pederson | Margaret Stock | Edward M. Uehling

Boston   Columbus   Indianapolis   New York   San Francisco   Upper Saddle River
Amsterdam   Cape Town   Dubai   London   Madrid   Milan   Munich   Paris   Montreal   Toronto
Delhi   Mexico City   Sao Paulo   Sydney   Hong Kong   Seoul   Singapore   Taipei   Tokyo

Pearson Resources for Instructors: *Diagnostic and Editing Tests and Exercises to accompany Pearson 2011 English Handbooks, Thirteenth Edition*

Copyright © 2011, 2010, 2009, 2008 Pearson Education, Inc.

1 2 3 4 5 6 7 8 9 10–BRR–13 12 11 10

www.pearsonhighered.com

ISBN-10: 0-205-82545-1

ISBN-13: 978-0-205-82545-5

CONTENTS

Description of the Materials in this Instructors' Supplemental Text

This instructors' supplemental text to Pearson handbooks contains eight diagnostic tests and twenty-four exercises—objective tests and exercises of grammatical, mechanical, and sentence structure skills—with answers keyed to these 2011 copyright English handbooks: *The Little, Brown Handbook, Brief Edition (LB Brief),* Fourth Edition (Aaron); *The Longman Handbook for Writers and Readers,* Sixth Edition (Anson/Schwegler); *The Writer's Handbook for College and Career*, (Dees/McManus/ Schwegler); *The New Century Handbook,* Fifth Edition (Hult/Huckin); *The Scott, Foresman Handbook for Writers,* Ninth Edition (Ruszkiewicz/Friend/Seward/Hairston); *The Scott, Foresman Writer,* Fifth Edition (Ruszkiewicz/Seward/Friend/Hairston); *The DK Handbook* and *The DK Handbook with Exercises,* both second editions (Wysocki/Lynch). Also included are answers to the questions with a classification of the skills tested in these diagnostic tests, and below are directions for administering, scoring, and interpreting the diagnostic tests. All eight tests in the text have similar formats. Instructors who want to use these tests as pre- and post-tests may use any pair of tests.

The text also contains nine editing tests that approximate the editing students will have to do to their own work. Answers for the editing tests also are included in this text. These tests will provide either diagnostic information or practice in editing skills.

This text additionally contains a brief essay on using a writing sample to test writing ability. Instructors will find more information from The National Testing Network in Writing and from professional organizations, such as the National Council of Teachers of English. Because research on testing—its techniques and theory—is ongoing, instructors should use these resources to guide the development of the testing program.

The tests and exercises included in this instructors' supplemental text are also available in Pearson MyTest™. The Pearson MyTest™ is a powerful assessment generation program that helps instructors easily create and print tests and exercises. This instructor-friendly tool allows the instructor to edit questions, add headers or footers, scramble questions and answer choices, create multiple versions and quickly save as MS-Word™ or PDF documents. Please see your Pearson representative for access to this program.

Testing Procedures and Evaluation

Administering the Test

Each student will need a copy of the test. If the tests are to be machine-scored, each student will also need an appropriate pencil and answer sheet. If the tests are to be used for class discussion of grammatical issues, students may mark on their tests.

The directions to the test items are contained within each test. Each test has 50 questions and can be completed in a 50-minute period.

Scoring the Test

The test may be scored by hand or by machine if the school has facilities for machine scoring. An answer key is provided with references to the relevant sections of each of the designated handbooks.

Interpreting the Results

The tests are indicators of mastery of specific information and skills—grammatical, mechanical, and compositional. These tests are not measures of general writing ability since no norms or standards of performance exist for any of the tests. Instructors should go over the individual test to see whether the information tested reflects that covered in the courses.

Diagnostic

The test results can be used to determine what skills or information need to be taught to a class. Instructors should supplement the information from the tests with that gained from reading students' papers.

Placement

The scores may also be used as *one* piece of information to determine a student's placement. However, because the tests have not been normed and because they are not measures of writing ability, the tests should not be used as the sole means of placement of students in a writing class. In addition, scores on the test should be considered as a band of about six to eight points.

Instructors in any department will want to use these scores, then, as *one* tool of assessment; they will also want to use other tools—writing samples and editing tests—to determine each student's ability. They will want to evaluate the effectiveness of *all* of these tools in a department's placement process.

USING A WRITING SAMPLE

Approaches to the assessment of writing changed dramatically in the 1970s with the emergence of the process movement. Pioneers such as Donald Murray, Peter Elbow, and Ken Macrorie, to name a few, called for a revised composition classroom, one that not only invited students into authentic writing situations with real-world audiences and purposes but also gave them enough time and guidance to improve their process as writers. Emphasizing the craft of writing as well as the concept of a writerly identity, many instructors focused on students' self expression, originality, and self esteem—all difficult concepts to effectively and reliably assess. For the most part, traditional notions of grammatical and mechanical correctness were neglected.

By the late 1980s, however, most writing instructors agreed that there was more to improving the quality of student writing than an earnest dedication to "the process." Political dimensions were also surfacing. Lisa Delpit, for example, criticized the process movement for inadequately preparing minority students for full participation in spheres of social and professional life where the conventions of Standard English are expected. Others criticized the movement for failing to prepare students for high-stakes exit and entrance exams. Over time, some writing instructors drew from rhetoric or linguistics to supplement their process pedagogies; others turned to the cognitive and social rhetorics then emanating from Carnegie Mellon and abroad; and most found ways to effectively re-integrate grammatical and mechanical conventions of mainstream discourse into their teaching and assessment, especially after the publication of Connie Weaver's influential *Teaching Grammar in Context*.

Today, the profession remains animated by the continual challenge to balance the situational and contingent dimensions of writing quality with the more readily accessible features, such as competence in standard discursive conventions. This balancing is reflected in the 1995 position statement on writing assessment authored by the CCCC Committee on Assessment, the 2000 outcomes statement authored by the Council of Writing Program Administrators, and the many instances of the profession's preferred tool of measurement, the writing sample.

Instructors prefer the writing sample for many reasons, including the following:

* Developments in the methods and professional standards of scoring have increased the reliability of writing sample assessment (AERA, APA, and NCME).
* Writing samples allow teachers to assess important lower-order features of writing, such as grammar, in context (Hillocks and Smith).
* Writing samples allow teachers to assess important higher-order features of writing, such as genre recognition, rhetorical error, and organization (Bishop and Ostrom).
* Writing samples align well with larger institutional assessment projects, such as portfolio assessment (Yancey; Belanoff and Dickson).

Because of its popularity, you may need to develop a writing-sample test as part or all of your institution's measurement of students' writing ability. If so, the following sample writing prompts for an essay and the various references should make the process easier.

When developing a writing-sample test, first determine the following logistics regarding the testing itself: date, time, place, supplies, proctors, scoring methods, raters, training, and posting of results. Although your common sense will provide much of the direction you will need, you will find invaluable information in Edward M. White's 1998 book on evaluation, *Teaching and Assessing Writing*, published by Calendar Islands and distributed by Parlor Press. White's expertise and practicality make the book an excellent resource.

As you make arrangements for the testing, you and the other faculty will need to devise and test several possible essay questions or writing prompts. Here you will find the research of the past years helpful. For instance, on the issue of what kind of writing you want students to produce, the conventional choices have been arguments—considered more difficult—or narratives—considered less difficult. However, research by Rosemary Hake indicates that raters more often misjudge an essay of pure narration than they do an essay of narration incorporated into exposition, what James Kinneavy labels persuasive discourse (154). Thus, Hake advocates prompts that have students incorporate narration into exposition (examples of such writing prompts are at the end of this essay).

Other research indicates that the quality of student writing remains the same whether writing prompts ask for opinions about public issues or for introspection on the writers' lives, notes Gordon Brossell (171). Karen Greenberg's research at CUNY further suggests that differences in the wording of the prompts do not produce corresponding differences in the quality of written responses (qtd. in Brossell 170), a contradiction of traditional wisdom in the field. Finally, Brossell has found that students write best when prompts have a moderate level of rhetorical specification about purpose, audience, speaker, and subject, noting as well that these prompts should have "a short introductory statement followed by a charge to the writer" (173).

To summarize, research suggests that prompts can be on either personal or public topics, should incorporate narration into exposition, and should have a moderate level of specificity about the rhetorical situation. However, research indicates that the most critical factor in devising prompts is adequate testing before their use in a writing-sample test. Such testing detects unanticipated problems in wording, in interpretation, and in interest level (Brossell 171). Thus, you will want to begin developing and testing possible prompts for your writing-sample test as soon as possible. If you find it difficult to develop your own prompts, you may use the two that follow this essay. Developing your own prompts, however, is important because the process compels you and your committee to refine your criteria for your writing courses and for students' writing. For further assistance, please see the selected bibliography of essential assessment research at the end of this section.

Once you complete the testing itself, the formidable task of scoring the essays remains. In this process you will need to discuss what you want the test to accomplish. Do you want it to distinguish general levels of writing ability to place students into writing courses, or do you want it to diagnose specific writing problems? Your choice of scoring method will depend upon the purpose of the test and your own evaluation of the methods, about which extensive research and considerable controversy exist. The two most commonly used scoring methods are holistic scoring and primary-trait scoring. Both Miles Myers's and Edward White's books offer detailed explanations of holistic scoring. White contrasts holistic grading that is based on an impression of the paper as a whole, with the detailed, analytic marking of papers often used in a writing course (120–21). This holistic scoring is not merely an intuitive impression to a set of papers; it works only when readers are properly trained to rate essays and prepared to maintain standards throughout the scoring. Holistic grading, as White explains, produces a ranking of the essays written by a given group of students on a topic, thus enabling placement of students into writing courses of different levels of difficulty (120–21). Holistic scoring, however, does not provide a diagnosis of the kinds of writing problems students have. Primary-trait scoring does yield some diagnostic information. It shares basic premises with holistic scoring but can single out a trait to be evaluated or scored for each essay (White 120). Even primary-trait scoring, however, provides a very limited diagnosis of students' writing problems. Despite the limitations, both types of scoring are useful in placing students into various levels in writing classes. White provides criteria for both holistic and primary-trait scoring, while Myers focuses on criteria for holistic scoring. Although both authors provide criteria for scoring, they stress that such criteria will be those of the faculty devising the test. Thus, even if you use the prompts at the end of this essay, you will still want to develop the criteria for scoring the essays.

The discussion of scoring indicates the virtual impossibility of using writing-sample tests to yield thorough diagnostic information about students' writing. Although some research on modifying primary-trait scoring to increase the number of traits scored is encouraging, analytic scoring of essays is still too time-consuming to perform on a large scale. Thus, many researchers advocate use of a writing-sample test and an objective tool of measurement for the most thorough assessment of students' writing ability.

Whatever combination of tests you use to assess students' writing ability, the final step is record-keeping. The needs of the committee, the department, and your institution will guide you. White offers suggestions that you can consult as you develop your system.

Recent issues, for instance, have indicated two significant developments in testing. One is the use of multiple writing samples to measure students' writing ability. This development reflects the emphasis in composition on writing as a process of discovery and on the portfolio method of assessment. The second is the use of longer time periods—up to three hours—for a single testing session to allow for revision and the use of prewriting in a writing-sample test. You and your faculty will want to discuss both of these developments so that your writing-sample test and its scoring can reflect your own theories about writing.

Thus, this discussion and the tests in this packet are part of current efforts in the profession to link writing assessment to writing instruction. Because calls for accountability proliferate almost daily, those who know current composition theory, practice, and research must become involved in assessment at all levels—national, state, institutional, and classroom. When informed professionals link writing assessment to writing instruction, more effective instruction and a more coherent curriculum ultimately result.

Sample Writing Prompts

Listed below are two essay questions that you may wish to use or adapt for a writing-sample test.

1. You have fifty minutes to write and revise an essay for a friend or relative of your parents (favorite aunt, uncle, or family friend) in which you develop an idea on the following topic and support it with references to your own experience or to your reader's experience: How do families treat male and female children differently?

2. You have fifty minutes to write an essay for a favorite adult (teacher, coach, aunt, or uncle) in which you discuss the following topic by developing a central idea and supporting it with references to your own experience and to this adult's experience: What are two or three ways that your generation differs from your parents' generation?

Works Cited

American Educational Research Association (AERA), American Psychological Association (APA), and National Council on Measurement in Education (NCME). *Standards for Educational and Psychological Testing*. Washington, D.C.: AERA, 1999. Print.

Belanoff, Pat, and Marcia Dickson, eds. *Portfolios: Process and Product*. Portsmouth: Boynton/Cook, 1991. Print.

Bishop, Wendy, and Hans Ostrom, eds. *Genre and Writing: Issues, Arguments, Alternatives*. Portsmouth: Boynton/Book, 1997. Print.

Brossell, Gordon. "Current Research and Unanswered Questions in Writing Assessment." In *Writing Assessment: Issues and Strategies*. Ed. Karen L. Greenberg, Harvey S. Wiener, and Richard A. Donovan. New York: Longman, 1986. 168–82. Print.

CCCC Committee on Assessment. "Writing Assessment: A Position Statement." *CCCC* 46.3 (1995): 430–437. Print.

Council of Writing Program Administrators. "WPA Outcomes Statement for First-Year Composition." *WPA: Writing Program Administration* 23.1/2 (fall/winter 1999): 59–66. Print.

Delpit, Lisa. "Skills and Other Dilemmas of a Progressive Black Educator." *Harvard Education Review* 56.4 (1986): 379–385. Print.

Elbow, Peter. *Writing Without Teachers*. New York: Oxford UP, 1973. Print.

Greenberg, Karen L., Harvey S. Wiener, and Richard A. Donovan, eds. *Writing Assessment: Issues and Strategies*. New York: Longman, 1986. Print.

Hake, Rosemary. "How Do We Judge What They Write?" In *Writing Assessment: Issues and Strategies*. Ed. Karen L. Greenberg, Harvey S. Wiener, and Richard A. Donovan. New York: Longman, 1986. 153–67. Print.

Hillocks, G., Jr., & Smith, M. W. "Grammar and Usage." *Handbook of Research on Teaching the English Language Arts*. Eds. J. Flood, J. M. Jensen, D. Lapp, & J. R. Squire. New York: Macmillan, 1991. 591–603. Print.

Macrorie, Ken. *Writing to Be Read*. New York: Hayden, 1968. Print.

Murray, Donald. *A Writer Teaches Writing: A Practical Method of Teaching Composition*. Boston: Houghton Mifflin, 1968. Print.

Myers, Miles. *A Procedure for Writing Assessment and Holistic Scoring*. Urbana: ERIC and NCTE, 1980. Print.

Weaver, Constance. *Teaching Grammar in Context*. Portsmouth: Heinemann Boynton/Cook, 1996. Print.

White, Edward. *Teaching and Assessing Writing*. Portland: Calendar Island, 1998. Print.

Yancey, Kathleen Blake, ed. *Portfolios in the Writing Classroom: An Introduction*. Urbana: NCTE, 1992. Print.

Selected Bibliography

Allison, Libby, Lizbeth Bryant, and Maureen Hourigan, eds. *Grading in the Post-Process Classroom: From Theory to Practice*. Portsmouth: Boynton, 1997. Print.

Belanoff, Pat, and Marcia Dickson, eds. *Portfolios: Process and Product*. Portsmouth: Boynton/Cook, 1991. Print.

Bizzell, Patricia. "Cognition, Convention, and Certainty: What We Need to Know About Writing." *Academic Discourse and Critical Consciousness*. Pittsburgh: U of Pittsburgh P, 1992. Print.

Bizzell, Patricia. "Review: What Can We Know, What Must We Do, What Must We Hope: Writing Assessment." *College English* 31 (1987): 575–84. Print.

Brossell, Gordon, and Barbara Hoetker Ash. "An Experiment with the Wording of Essay Topics." *College Composition and Communication* 35 (1984): 423–25. Print.

CCCC Committee on Assessment. "Writing Assessment: A Position Statement." *CCCC* 46.3 (1995): 430–437. Print.

Cooper, Charles R., and Lee Odell, eds. *Evaluating Writing: Describing, Measuring, and Judging*. Urbana: NCTE, 1977. Print.

Council of Writing Program Administrators. "WPA Outcomes Statement for First-Year Composition." *WPA: Writing Program Administration* 23.1/2 (fall/winter 1999): 59–66. Print.

Designing Writing Tasks for the Assessment of Writing. Norwood: Ablex, 1987. Print.

Elbow, Peter. "Ranking, Evaluating, Liking: Sorting Out Three Forms of Judgment." *College English* 55 (1993): 187–206. Print.

Gorman, T.P., A.C. Purves, and R.E. Degenhart, eds. *The IEA Study of Written Composition: The International Writing Tasks and Scoring Scales.* Oxford: Pergamon, 1988. Print.

Greenberg, Karen L., Harvey S. Wiener, and Richard A. Donovan, eds. *Writing Assessment: Issues and Strategies.* New York: Longman, 1986. Print.

Gross, Barbara, Michael Scriven, and Susan Thomas. *The Evaluation of Composition Instruction.* 2nd ed. New York: Teachers College, 1987. Print.

Haswell, Richard. "Dark Shadows: The Fate of Writers at the Bottom." *College Composition and Communication 34* (1988): 303–16. Print.

Hillocks, G., Jr., & Smith, M. W. "Grammar and Usage." *Handbook of Research on Teaching the English Language Arts.* Eds. J. Flood, J. M. Jensen, D. Lapp, & J. R. Squire. New York: Macmillan, 1991. 591–603. Print.

Hoetker, James, and Gordon Brossell. "A Procedure for Writing Content-Fair Essay *Examination Topics* for Large-Scale Writing Assessments." *College Composition and Communication* 37 (1986): 328–35. Print.

Myers, Miles. *A Procedure for Writing Assessment and Holistic Scoring.* Urbana: ERIC and NCTE, 1980. Print.

Purves, Alan. "In Search of an *Internationally Valid Scheme* for Scoring Compositions." *College Composition and Communication* 35 (1984): 426–38. Print.

Ruth, Leo, and Sandra Murphy. "Designing Topics for Writing Assessment: Problems of Meaning." *College Composition and Communication* 35 (1984): 410–22. Print.

Stock, Patricia L., and Francelia Clark. "Researching Practice: Evaluating Assessment Essays." *College Composition and Communication* 37 (1986): 315–27. Print.

Weaver, Constance. *Teaching Grammar in Context.* Portsmouth: Heinemann Boynton/Cook, 1996. Print.

White, Edward M. "Holisticism." *College Composition and Communication* 35 (1984): 400–09. Print.

White, Edward. *Teaching and Assessing Writing*. Portland: Calendar Island, 1998. Print.

White, Edward. *Assigning, Responding, Evaluating*. New York: Bedford/St. Martin's Press, 1999. Print.

Wolcott, Willa, Sue M. Legg. *An Overview of Writing Assessment: Theory, Research, and Practice*. Urbana: National Council of Teachers of English, 1998. Print.

Wolcott, Willa. "Writing Instruction and Assessment: The Need for Interplay Between Process and Product." *College Composition and Communication* 38 (1987): 40–46. Print.

Yancey, Kathleen Blake, ed. *Portfolios in the Writing Classroom: An Introduction*. Urbana: NCTE, 1992. Print.

Zak, Frances and Christopher C. Weaver, eds. *The Theory and Practice of Grading Writing: Problems and Possibilities*. Albany: SUNY Press, 1998. Print.

Editing Tests

Editing Test I

*Edit the following passages for comma splices, sentence fragments, and run-ons **only**. Each entry may have more than one error.*

1) The waves pounding on the stern of the small green sailboat. Then it rounded the sharp curve in the bay so the wind and current now were flowing together. The two pushed the small craft safely home into its own small inlet.

2) A popular person in our small community is my friend Clara. Readily recognized because of her amazing laugh. Its power and infectious delight never cease to captivate me.

3) The middle-aged woman startled all her friends. Who gaped in disbelief as she quit her job, broke off her engagement, and moved halfway across the country to start a new life. Surprisingly, she's happy, sometimes rash moves are good ones.

4) Shaney and Tannie seem alike in many ways, both earn good grades and have quick, zany senses of humor. Tannie, however, loves sports and the outdoors while Shaney prefers lying on the couch to read novels or to watch videos.

5) John and his friends from high school decided to take a month-long camping trip across the country last August. Because they had finished college and were moving to different parts of the country. Amazingly, John's '72 Cutlass made the trip safely.

Editing Test II

*Edit the following passage. Correct any errors in capitalization, spelling, and punctuation. Divide the passage into paragraphs. Make **only** essential changes.*

1)   When my husband Joe had cancer surgery five years ago, each of his family members responded just as I knew they would. John, his father, decided to organize the family's calls. Because, of course, everything would run so much more smoothly. Thus Jane, Matt, and Jim recieved detailed sheets of instructions in the mail. Telling them which days to telephone r.j. smith hospital to talk to Joe and what presents to send. Jane, enraged, promptly threw a tantrum. Calling Matt and me to complain about her father's overbearing behavior. "I," she yelled, "am a Psychiatrist who knows how to handle these situations, i am not still a child." Matt also responded predictably. By avoiding the situation. He threw himself into his work. Normally a late sleeper, Matt took to leaving at 5:00 a.m., driving on the deserted expressway and arriving at work before six a.m. In addition, he didn't return until 11:00 p.m. When he would fall into bed so exhausted that he couldn't worry about Joe. Jim, too, responded predictably. He fumed inside for weeks, ignored John's instructions, and sent cartons of books to Joe. So that he would never be bored. The books were funny. Because Jim had read Norman Cousins' book about the healing power of laughter. Within a few months, Joe recovered from the surgery-in spite of his family.

Editing Test III

*Edit the following passage. Correct any errors in capitalization, spelling, and punctuation. Divide the passage into paragraphs. Make **only** essential changes.*

1)   Voice lessons have not met my expectations. I thought professor rosman's methods, goals, and repertoire would be predictable and stuffy. Not startling and thorughly unconventional. I knew rosman's methods were unusual at my first lesson in setember of 1990. When he asked me to pretend that I could only make grunts and had no control of my jaw muscles. Another time I had to say "Unique New York" as I went sang scales. At one lesson I even had to sing all my songs with "brr" as my only word. Rosman's goals for me were not, to my releif, to make me sound like an opera singer. Because I wanted to sound like a torch singer. Like Linda Ronstadt with the Nelson Riddle orchestra. Rosman wanted me to enjoy singing. To support my voice with good air flow, and to sing the words as I would speak them. He didn't make me sing opera or art songs. Although I did like the italian and french songs I sang. I sang songs that streched my voice's range and songs that I liked. Songs such as "Can't Help loving That Man of Mine" and "September song." My favorites were "The Water is wide," a folk song that James Taylor has recorded, and "Amazing Grace," a song that Judy Collins has recorded. Voice lessons have been fun. Not what I expected.

Editing Test IV

*Edit the following passage. Correct any errors in capitalization, spelling, and punctuation. Divide the passage into paragraphs. Make **only** essential changes.*

1) Mary Strong is a librarian. Who is called Mary Prunella Clapsaddle Jones by her close friends. Because she collects strange names as other people collect rare stamps. Petite and pretty, she is witty, kind, and startlingly frank.

2) Marian and Matt are lifelong enemies. Because they are so much alike. She is bright, competitive, and energetic, he prides himself on his intellectual ability, his innate superiority, and his persistence. Whenever the two are together, fireworks flare.

3) Marooned on the mud flat, our skiff was useless for the next few hours. Until the tide came in. We sat on the bank, swatted mosquitos, and sniped at each other. We were not happy campers.

4) The wind streaming around the tall buildings, roaring down the empty cross streets. Its force lifted my loose shoe and flung it into the rain-soaked street. I was shocked and shoeless in Chicago.

5) When she was nineteen, she joined the Dolphin Players. Which produced quality plays in various small theaters in the city. She remained active in the group until she was twenty-five. When she moved to New York City to become a professional actress.

Editing Test V

*Edit the following passage. Correct any errors in capitalization, spelling, and punctuation. Divide the passage into paragraphs. Make **only** essential changes.*

1)   My first sailing trip taught me two valuable lesons. First I realized that I always needed to take extra provisions. When we set out, the sky was blue and cloudless, the breeze was warm. We ate our picnic lunch within the first hour. Then we sailed for two more hours. All the way up shinglehouse slough. When we headed home, we realized that the tide had alredy turned and that we had to hurry, however, the wind had died. We decided to row. We rowed until we were near charleston bridge. Where the boat snagged on a mud flat. John and I piled out and started to push the boat through the shallow water. Hurrying to get to the deeper channel before the tide was completely out. The sun was now gone, fog and wind were swirling around the boat. We wanted more food and warmer clothing, both were at home, not in the boat. Then I learned my second lesson nature is powerful. As we reached deeper water, we realized that the waves were growing steadily higher. Although the fog was beginning to lift. Soon we were surfing on top of the waves in our little skiff. Propelled by the wind and the current. I began comparing how far I could swim with how far away the shore was. I sat huddled in the bottom of the boat. In an inch of water from the waves' spray. Finally, we nosed the boat into the narrow inlet. We scrambled out. Mother nature was a tough teacher.

Editing Test VI

*Edit the following passage. Correct any errors in capitalization, spelling, and punctuation. Divide the passage into paragraphs. Make **only** essential changes.*

1)   When Muriel decided to take up smoking a cigar. she shocked her friends and family, also she horrified her husband Arnold. Because everyone disapproved of her cigar smoking, Muriel began to avoid her friends, family, and husband. Instead, she started to research the history of cigars, furthermore, she began to hang around the local cigar stores on broadway avenue. There she met some fascinating people. Who had knowledge of the wide variety of cigars produced around the world. If Muriel wanted to know about Russian cigars she asked josef asknessazy questions, however, if she wanted to understand why cuban cigars were considered so fine, she asked juan canolos. After she had hung around the cigar shops for months, had read twenty books, and had read the last five years' issues of Puff, Muriel felt she knew enough about cigars to defend her habit to anyone. Furthermore, she decided to open her own cigar shop in her neighborhood. Arnold agreed. So that he could see more of her. The two opened a small cigar store a few months later. Muriel worked hard, she found a suitable vacant building for the new store. Arnold helped her secure the loan, moreover, he was a cosigner. The two cleaned the building, repainted it, and rented the necessary furniture. They now own a thriving business in the heart of portland. Muriel and Arnold are an American success story.

Editing Test VII

*Edit the following passages for comma splices, sentence fragments, and run-ons **only**. Each entry may have more than one error.*

1) The wind howling in the scraggly trees and barren bushes. Then it stopped and the pounding rains started, they went on for the next forty hours without diminishing in force.

2) Kate Smith was a famous singer. Known for her rendition of "God Bless America" and for her propensity for accidents. During the latter years of her life she broke one leg twice by falling in the same hotel ballroom.

3) Joan and Rich are two friends who are both characters in different ways, Joan is totally outrageous in her behavior and will say and do anything, while Rich is witty, but not courageous.

4) Physical injuries can produce innovative adaptations. A good friend, who was a professional potter, had to give up pottery when her spine was injured. Because she couldn't apply the pressure necessary to center and hold the clay in place. Now she is a first-rate quilter, showing her work in galleries across thenation.

5) The recent rash of air-traffic controller errors prompted an investigation by the FAA. Which found that most errors were a result of pilots and controllers not being able to understand each other's words. The FAA made a startling recommendation: voice training for both groups.

Editing Test VIII

*Edit the following passage. Correct any errors in capitalization, spelling, and punctuation. Divide the passage into paragraphs. Make **only** essential changes.*

1)   Winifred, my aunt, had a great fondness for hard cider. As the British call it. She was quite a law-abiding lady, with hair pulled back in a bun and hose with very straight seams, prim in most respects. Until the aroma of hard cider filled her nostrils. Then she would lift one of her carefully tweezed eyebrows ever so slightly, murmur a vague but polite excuse to those present, and head directly for the cider. The family all of whom knew these alarming symptoms only too well immediately would launch their individual strategic maneuvers. To divert her attention from the cider. Uncle Bob a man who hated confrontation and who loved mysteries usually began his own campaign to find the cider source first. Before she found it. Aunt martha was more direct, she would grab Winifred's arm with the force of a well-muscled wrestler and pull her toward the kitchen for a "friendly talk." Uncle John was the cagiest, therefore he was the most successful. With utmost discretion infinite patience and resolute determination he would trail Winifred. As if he had no particular interest in where or what she was doing, then he would just happen to engage her in a heated conversation on her favorite topic: the royal society for the prevention of cruelty to animals. Because of these strategies, the family managed to keep Winifreds cider consumption to a minimum. Until the fateful summer of 1979. The swill summer we called it later.

Editing Test IX

*Edit the following passage. Correct any errors in capitalization, spelling, and punctuation. Divide the passage into paragraphs. Make **only** essential changes.*

1)   Racquetball is my favorite sport, so I play it two or three times a week. Except for the weeks of midterms and finals. I play with two boys and one girl. We usually play at the John G. and Jane J. Brown recreational center. You have to pay two dollars for the court, even if your a member. Some kids think that's awful, but I think its fair. Tuesdays I play with Joe my neighbor and classmate. He's a wild and crazy guy on the courts. Swinging wildly and forcefully he hits the ball so hard sometimes that it makes a whistling noise. As it zooms past me to smack into the wall. Although we have played racquetball together for two years I have yet to return one of those killer balls. My other steady partner is Conrad. A friend who used to play tennis competitively. Conrad plays only for the fun of the game. My own game has improved dramatically since we began playing together a year ago. Because I've learned how to catch the ball as it comes off the wall and how to serve the ball so that its almost unreturnable. Last spring I learned the drop and the half-volley shots. Now our games are more fun for both of us. My other partner Shirley is learning to play racquetball so we just volley for an hour. Although Shirley used to play tennis she hasn't played for a long time, thus her game is rusty. Our practice has improved her game. Playing with all three is great fun and great exercise.

Diagnostic Tests

DIAGNOSTIC TEST A

MULTIPLE CHOICE. Choose the one alternative that best completes the statement or answers the question.

1) We chose the _____ of the two remaining videos in the rental store for the children's party.
    A) better   B) best

2) Neither her associates nor the doctor _____ the surgery is necessary.
    A) thinks   B) think

3) Do you really want to give _____ the money that you earned?
    A) she and Jim   B) Jim and she
    C) Jim and her   D) them two

4) The sick old man _____ eat his dinner.
    A) could hardly   B) couldn't hardly

5) Each cat in the four-state cat show had _____ own elaborate display area.
    A) it's   B) its
    C) their   D) there

6) United is one of the domestic airlines that _____ applied to the FAA to carry overseas traffic.
    A) has   B) have

7) I _____ to bed two hours before it started raining.
    A) had went B) went   C) had gone

8) The doctor said that both you and _____ must make immediate changes in order to reduce the possibility of heart disease.
    A) he   B) him   C) them

9) The sleek brown seals did not know what had ruined _____ breeding grounds when the oil washed onto the beaches.
    A) they're B) there   C) their

10) Johnny's best friend wondered why he was doing _____ in his science courses since he had been an A student for years.

      A) bad   B) badly

11) The coach gave the swim team two extra hours to gather _____ tickets and suitcases for the trip to the swimming meet.

      A) their   B) his   C) her   D) its

12) I don't have any idea what you _____ doing out that night.

      A) were   B) we're   C) where

13) The NFL teams that I dislike the most _____ the Dallas Cowboys, the Cleveland Browns, and the Jacksonville Jaguars.

      A) are,   B) are   C) are: D) are;

14) Would the holder of ticket number 08537 please do the _____ go to the main lobby information desk to claim your prize.

      A) following   B) following,
      C) following;   D) following:

15) The doctor carefully _____ the precise side effects of the drug, as well as its potential benefits.

      A) suggested   B) explained
      C) implied   D) alluded to

16) Because his father _____ his ten-speed bike away to punish him for his failing grades, the boy sulked for two days.

      A) took   B) taken   C) had took   D) had taken

17) If I _____ to my father, I would not be in prison today.

      A) would of listened   B) woulda listened
      C) had listened   D) would have listened

18) His sister is the only one of his seemingly endless friends and acquaintances who _____ offered to help him after he contracted meningitis.

      A) has   B) have

19) I _____ him do it yesterday.

      A) seen   B) saw   C) have seen   D) had seen

20) At the international conference, the scientists had to defend the _____ points of their research.
      A) principal   B) principle

21) The young boy ran over to give his sad uncle a hug because he knew the uncle felt _____.
      A) bad   B) badly

22) To sustain good health, _____ important to follow a healthful diet.
      A) its   B) its'   C) it's

23) She graduated from _____.
      A) High School   B) High school
      C) Washington high school   D) Washington High School

24) I pulled two _____ at the same time.
      A) cat's tails   B) cats' tails
      C) cat's tails'   D) cats tail's

25) We knew who had been elected chairman, but we did not yet know _____ he had appointed to fill the various vacancies in the standing committee.
      A) who   B) whom

26) Which sentence is the most correct, clear, and concise?
      A) In order to achieve a life that is both successful and rewarding, individuals must focus on developing one set of skills that they can sell and many outside interests.
      B) In order to live a life that is both successful and rewarding, one must develop a particular skill that is in demand by the marketplace and diverse outside interests to amuse one throughout life.
      C) For a successful, rewarding life, an individual must develop a marketable skill and diverse interests.
      D) To have a successful, rewarding life, individuals must develop particular, marketable skills, and they also must explore diverse interests.

27) Which sentence is the most correct, clear and concise?
      A) Of the catastrophic airplane crash on the late-night news we heard.
      B) We heard of the catastrophic air crash on the late-night news.
      C) On the late-night news, we heard about the catastrophic airplane crash.

28) Which sentence is the most correct, clear, and concise?
    A) The decision to be honest about her own needs in the relationship was made by Jane.
    B) The decision about the need for her to be honest about her own needs in the relationship was made by Jane.
    C) Jane decided to be honest about her own needs in the relationship.
    D) The decision was made by Jane to be honest about her own needs in the relationship.

29) Which sentence is the most correct, clear, and concise?
    A) My son has learned responsibility by having a dog, learning to take care of it, and giving it consistent care.
    B) Having a dog has helped my son who has to learn, by this experience, how to take care of his new pet and how consistent he must be in giving it the care that all new pets, young or old, need from their owners.
    C) Having a dog, learning to take care of it, and because it requires consistent care teach my son responsibility.

30) Which sentence is the most correct, clear, and concise?
    A) The adolescent's dominant mood was one of intense exhilaration.
    B) The youth most often felt a sense of excitement about the manifold possibilities inherent in life.
    C) The immature person's preponderant emotional state was one of extreme excitement.
    D) The teenager was often excited.

31) Which sentence is the most correct, clear, and concise?
    A) In the world's society of today, what most people agree is needed is some sort of decisive action.
    B) Today we need prompt action.
    C) At this point in time there is a need for swift, prompt action.
    D) In this modern world of today, what is needed is immediate action.

32) Which sentence is the most correct, clear, and concise?
    A) The Statue of Liberty made me aware of the importance of this symbol of our country standing on the bottom of the steps to the torch.
    B) Standing on the bottom of the steps to the torch of the Statue of Liberty, I realized the importance of this symbol of our country.
    C) Standing on the bottom of the steps to the torch, the Statue of Liberty made me aware of the importance of this symbol of our country.

33) Which sentence is the most correct, clear, and concise?
   A) In our present day and time, on the anniversary of the World Trade Center attack, federal officials have indicated clearly that they have new rules and procedures to prevent another attack of that magnitude.
   B) Today, the anniversary of the World Trade Center attack, federal officials stressed that they have instituted stricter procedures to prevent another attack.
   C) At this moment of the anniversary of the World Trade Center attack, the officials of the federal government forcefully stressed that they have put into place a series of tougher regulations and procedures to prevent another such catastrophic tragedy.
   D) On this day, the anniversary of the World Trade Center attack, the federal government administration put emphasis on the fact that they have new regulations to prevent another such catastrophic tragedy.

34) Which sentence is the most correct, clear, and concise?
   A) Doctors must work hard to care for their patients.
   B) Every doctor must work hard to care for their patients.
   C) All doctors must work hard to care for his patients.
   D) A doctor must work hard to care for their patients.

35) Which sentence is the most correct, clear, and concise?
   A) We asked every girl who plays on the team for her opinion.
   B) We asked every girl, who plays on the team, for her opinion.
   C) We asked every girl who plays on the team for their opinion.
   D) We asked every girl, who plays on the team, for their opinion.

SHORT ANSWER. Write the word or phrase that best completes each statement or answers the question.
Choose the sentence that best expresses the relationship between the two clauses.

36)
   A. Sara is both a creative and disciplined writer; **however**, she won a prize for writing the most innovative mystery series of the decade.
   B. Sara is both a creative and disciplined writer; **as a result**, she won a prize for writing the most innovative mystery series of the decade.
   C. Sara is both a creative and disciplined writer; **nonetheless**, she won a prize for writing the most innovative mystery series of the decade.
   D. Sara is both a creative and disciplined writer; **otherwise**, she won a prize for writing the most innovative mystery series of the decade.

37)
    A. Dave twisted his ankle during the second mile of the marathon; **consequently**, he finished the race.
    B. Dave twisted his ankle during the second mile of the marathon; **likewise**, he finished the race.
    C. Dave twisted his ankle during the second mile of the marathon; **nevertheless**, he finished the race.
    D. Dave twisted his ankle during the second mile of the marathon; **therefore**, he finished the race.

One of the four underlined sections may mark an error in punctuation. Choose the letter that marks the error in punctuation. If there is no error, choose E.

38) Often it is difficult to get along with <u>another, for</u> each person often has different
                                                   A

expectations in a relationship. In two cases involving friends of

<u>mine, relationships</u> seemed to go smoothly for the first six <u>weeks, however,</u> the
     B   C
next six weeks brought frequent misunderstandings. The friends found that they

had to alter their <u>expectations,</u> that they had to work on the relationship, and
                              D
that they had to talk about any misunderstandings immediately. <u>No error.</u>
                                                          E

39) Lake <u>Michigan, which</u> stretches all along the eastern edge of Chicago, <u>Illinois,</u> is
              A   B
beautiful but dangerous. Dr. Janet <u>Mathus, a</u> noted authority on the Great Lakes,
                                         C
reports that within the twenty-four-hour period of June 14, <u>1989, the</u> lake claimed
                                                               D
the lives of twenty-two people in fifteen different accidents. <u>No error.</u>
                                                        E

40) For most of us who are not reading <u>specialists, learning</u> to read is a mysterious
                                        A

<u>process; why</u> a child is ready to learn to read one week and not two weeks earlier is
    B

a puzzle. <u>Although, the</u> process of learning to read is <u>perplexing,</u> experts are
           C   D

conducting research that promises to unravel the mysteries, thereby suggesting

ways to help children learn to read. <u>No error.</u>
                                        E

One of the four underlined sections may mark an error in capitalization. Choose the
letter that marks the error in punctuation. If there is no error, choose E.

41) During the Vietnam <u>War,</u> some families were split apart when some sons went to
                        A

fight, while others went <u>north</u> to Canada to escape the draft. Twenty years later
                          B

<u>psychiatrists</u> work with <u>Veterans</u> to heal their psychic scars. <u>No error.</u>
     C   D   E

42) For my birthday last <u>spring,</u> I went to New York City, New York, and explored the
                          A

<u>American</u> <u>Craft</u> Museum, which had shows on interlacing, contemporary
    B   C

<u>European</u> glass works, and recent acquisitions. <u>No error.</u>
    D   E

In each of the following sets, identify the example that illustrates a fragment, run-on (or
fused) sentence, or comma splice.

43)
        A. Help!
        B. Especially when I'm tired from working at the grocery store all night without
           any help.
        C. Run for your life!
        D. Get serious!

44)
        A. The doorbell rang, so I went to answer it.
        B. The doorbell rang; I answered it.
        C. The doorbell rang I answered it.
        D. When the doorbell rang, I answered it.

45)

    A. Remember to think of others as well as yourself.
    B. Remember it is not just you, think of others as well.
    C. Remember it is not just you; think of others too.
    D. Remember it is not only you. Think of others also.

46)

    A. I call long distance on Sundays, then I am more likely to find someone at home.
    B. I call long distance on Sundays, for I am more likely to find someone at home.
    C. I call long distance on Sundays because I am more likely to find someone at home.
    D. I call long distance on Sundays; I am more likely to find someone at home.

47)

    A. In Uno there is the *skip card* this is also a common card.
    B. In Uno there is the *skip card*, also a common card.
    C. There is also the *skip card*, a common card in Uno.
    D. The game of Uno has a common card called the *skip card*.

48)

    A. After you get a good night's sleep, you should be ready for a productive day.
    B. You should be ready for a productive day after you get a good night's sleep.
    C. You are more likely to have a productive day after getting a good night's sleep.
    D. After you get a good night's sleep. You should be ready for a productive day.

49)

    A. The oven setting placed to bake.
    B. Place the setting to bake.
    C. You should set the oven to bake.
    D. First, set the oven to bake.

50)

    A. Monday's workout will consist of bench presses, squats, and curls.
    B. Monday's workout will consist of lifts. They include bench presses, squats, and curls.
    C. Monday's workout will consist of three lifts. Bench presses, squats, and curls.
    D. Monday's workout will consist of three lifts: bench presses, squats, and curls.

DIAGNOSTIC TEST B

MULTIPLE CHOICE. Choose the one alternative that best completes the statement or answers the question.

1) I am not sure why you _____ doing that.
    A) where   B) we're   C) were

2) Each horse in the race had _____ colors.
    A) their   B) there   C) its D) it's

3) The young lawyer struggled to understand and to articulate the _____ of the complex case.
    A) principal B) principle

4) The old man is one of many individuals who _____ lost their life savings to those crooks.
    A) has   B) have

5) The ballerina felt _____, for she did not know the choreography well.
    A) badly   B) bad

6) Do you really have to give _____ the best chocolates from the box?
    A) Al and she   B) Al and her   C) she and Al

7) After the news of his friend's death in the car crash, Jeff wished that he _____ his friends not to drive when they were drunk.
    A) would've warned   B) would of warned
    C) had warned   D) would warn

8) Of the four children, she was the _____ generous.
    A) most   B) more

9) _____ impressive to see a grizzly bear in the wild.
    A) Its'   B) Its   C) It's

10) Neither the majorettes nor the drum major _____ to alter the routine.
    A) want   B) wants

31

11) In her column, the reviewer wrote that the ballet dancers _____ a wonderful performance.

      A) had given   B) had gave   C) gave

12) Students in the summer art class were involved enough in _____ work to skip lunch to complete a project.

      A) his   B) her   C) their

13) Our home was damaged by the storm _____ we will have to replace our roof.

      A) so,   B) , so;   C) , so,   D) , so

14) In a fit of anger after an argument, I _____ out all of my friend's letters and pictures.

      A) threw   B) had thrown   C) thru   D) through

15) Louis was a scoundrel _____ everyone distrusted.

      A) who   B) whom

16) The government official carefully _____ the precise responsibilities of each new cabinet officer.

      A) explained   B) implied
      C) alluded to   D) inferred

17) After the committee had deliberated, they _____ a report that included the concerns of the citizens.

      A) wrote   B) had wrote   C) written   D) had written

18) The lawyer suggested that you and _____ work to find an agreement outside the courtroom, for the trial would be long and unpleasant.

      A) his   B) he   C) him

19) The pressure to complete all of the work weighed _____ upon her mind.

      A) heavy   B) heavily

20) The dancing instructor told the class to practice in order to make _____ steps automatic.

      A) their   B) its

21) The committee found it difficult to _____ his revisions.
   A) accept   B) except

22) Alan's friends resented him because they were not as talented as _____.
   A) he   B) him   C) his

23) At the dog show, the _____ exhibited great concentration in determining the winner of each category.
   A) dogs' judges'   B) dogs' judges
   C) dog's judges   D) dogs judges

24) The ambulance responded to an accident at the construction _____.
   A) cite   B) sight   C) site

25) The sophomores _____ contain their excitement at having won first place in the university's academic contest.
   A) could hardly   B) couldn't hardly

26) Which sentence is the most correct, clear, and concise?
   A) The association gave the award to the lawyers who won the most cases for his or her clients.
   B) The association gave the award to the lawyers who won the most cases for clients.
   C) The association gave the award to the lawyer who won the most cases for their clients.

27) Which sentence is correct, clear, and concise?
   A) Joan will make an effective president of the class, for she has intelligence, perseverance, dedication, and humor.
   B) Joan will be the best person to be president of the class because she has such fine intelligence, her ability to persevere is clear, she possesses a basic sense of determination, and a lovely sense of humor.
   C) Joan will be an excellent class president because she has intelligence, a sense of humor, an extraordinary strong inner sense that enables her to persevere, and a sense of dedication.

28) Which sentence is correct, clear, and concise?
   A) Walking on the stone wall three feet above the water, Lake Michigan reminds me of the power and untamed beauty of nature.
   B) Lake Michigan reminds me of the power and untamed beauty of nature walking on the stone wall three feet above the water.
   C) Walking on the stone wall three feet above the water of Lake Michigan, I appreciate the power and untamed beauty of nature.

29) Which sentence is correct, clear, and concise?
   A) The senior citizen's principal mood was one of irritation.
   B) The octogenarian experienced constant irritation about the limitations of his mental ability.
   C) The old man was usually irritable.
   D) The elderly person's predominant mental condition was one of extreme irritation.

30) Which sentence is correct, clear, and concise?
   A) My son, by the very experience of having a newspaper route, has learned the responsibility that comes with a job and how much he must discipline himself.
   B) Having a newspaper route, learning responsibility, and to acquire discipline teach my son how to handle a job.
   C) My son has learned how to handle a job by having a newspaper route, discipline, and practicing responsibility.

31) Which sentence is correct, clear, and concise?
   A) The choice to go to the college that she liked best was made by Katherine.
   B) Katherine chose to go to the college she liked most.
   C) The choice about which college she liked most was made by Katherine herself.
   D) The choice to go to the college that was most appealing to her was made by Katherine.

32) Which sentence is correct, clear, and concise?
   A) The plumbers replaced the water lines with plastic pipe that were leaking.
   B) The plumbers replaced the leaking water lines with plastic pipe.
   C) With plastic pipe the water lines that were leaking were replaced by the plumbers.

33) Which sentence is correct, clear, and concise?
   A) To discover, to understand, and to create-these are the activities of the educated.
   B) The activities of educated people are to discover, understand, and creation.
   C) To discover, understand, and creation are the activities of the educated.
   D) To discover, to understand, and to create; these are the activities of the educated.

34) Which sentence is correct, clear, and concise?
   A) The committee argued about seat belt legislation and they could not scarcely remain polite.
   B) The committee argued about seat belt legislation and it could scarcely remain polite.
   C) The committee argued about seat belt legislation, and it could not scarcely remain polite.
   D) The committee argued about seat belt legislation, and they could scarcely remain polite.

35) Which sentence best expresses the relationship between the two clauses?
   A) Looking at the character development in the story, the novelist reveals to us surprisingly psychological insight.
   B) Looking at the character development in the story, we discover the novelist's surprisingly psychological insight.
   C) Looking at the character development in the story, surprising psychological insight is revealed to us.
   D) Looking at the character development in the story, the novelist surprisingly reveals psychological insight to us.

36) Which sentence best expresses the relationship between the two clauses?
   A) Jane is a pretty girl with a good sense of humor and a quick intelligence, but she is shy and has difficulty making friends.
   B) Jane is a pretty girl with a good sense of humor and a quick intelligence. Then she is shy and has difficulty making friends.
   C) Jane is a pretty girl with a good sense of humor and a quick intelligence; therefore, she is shy and has difficulty making friends.

37) Which sentence best expresses the relationship between the two clauses?
   A) He is bright, hard working, and agreeable; <u>moreover</u>, he is attractive and punctual.
   B) He is bright, hard working, and agreeable; <u>thus</u>, he is attractive and punctual.
   C) He is bright, hard working, and agreeable; <u>nonetheless</u>, he is attractive and punctual.

One of the underlined sections may mark an error in punctuation. Choose the letter that marks the error in punctuation. If there is no error, choose E.

38) Moving to a new city is often both stressful and <u>exciting, for</u> although we are
                                                              A
<u>isolated, we</u> are faced with possibilities. For most average <u>adults, the</u> first six
     B   C
months are stressful. The next six months bring the comfort of new

<u>friendships, the</u> adventure of new places, and the satisfaction of making a new
          D
home. <u>No error</u>.
           E

39) On certain days I seem to go at the world in the wrong <u>direction.</u> I feel clumsy,
                                                                 A
unintelligent, irritable, and <u>depressed, others</u> seem overbearing, arrogant, clever,
                                    B
and <u>insufferable. On</u> such <u>days I</u> try to retreat to a quiet place as soon as possible.
           C   D
<u>No error</u>.
     E

40) In the midst of great personal <u>happiness, some</u> people have difficulty empathizing
                                          A
with another person who is in <u>pain; we</u> often fear feeling another's pain.
                                     B
<u>Nevertheless, we</u> can find ways to help each <u>other; if</u> we are willing to do so.
        C   D
<u>No error</u>.
     E

One of the four underlined words in this passage may mark an error in capitalization. Choose the letter that marks the error in capitalization. If there is no error, write E.

41) During the Vietnam <u>war</u>, some families experienced turmoil when one son went
                          A
<u>north</u> to Canada to avoid the draft and one went <u>east</u> for training before being
   B   C
shipped to Vietnam to fight. Many <u>clinical</u> psychiatrists have tried to explain the
                                        D
divisions within these families. <u>No error</u>.
                                       E

42) For vacation I went to Fort Worth, Texas, and explored the <u>Amon</u> <u>Carter</u> <u>Museum</u>
                                                   A   B   C

that had shows on Winslow Homer, contemporary <u>American</u> photography, and
                                                     D

recent acquisitions. <u>No error</u>.
                              E

43) Which of the following examples illustrates a fragment, run-on (or fused) sentence, or comma splice?
     A) The band was ready to leave, but the car would not start.
     B) The band was ready to leave; however, the car would not start.
     C) Although the band was ready to leave, the car would not start.
     D) The band was ready to leave, the car, however, would not start.

44) Which of the following examples illustrates a fragment, run-on (or fused) sentence, or comma splice?
     A) As the band walked to work, Elwood composed a song called "Cadillac Blues."
     B) Elwood composed a song called "Cadillac Blues" as the band walked to work.
     C) Although Elwood composed a song called "Cadillac Blues" as the band walked to work.
     D) The band walked to work; incidentally, Elwood composed a song called "Cadillac Blues."

45) Which of the following examples illustrates a fragment, run-on (or fused) sentence, or comma splice?
     A) The band was late for its gig; indeed, the bar was just closing when they arrived.
     B) The band was so late for its gig that the bar was just closing when they arrived.
     C) The band arrived late, not surprisingly, the bar was just closing when they arrived.
     D) When the band-late again-arrived for its gig, the bar was just closing.

46) Which of the following examples illustrates a fragment, run-on (or fused) sentence, or comma splice?
     A) Stretching and yawning, Elwood went to sleep on a pool table.
     B) Elwood, stretching and yawning, went to sleep on a pool table.
     C) Elwood stretched and yawned, then he went to sleep on a pool table.
     D) Elwood stretched, yawned, and then went to sleep on a pool table.

47) Which of the following examples illustrates a fragment, run-on (or fused) sentence, or comma splice?
    A) "Get off that pool table," shouted the bartender the next morning, "get out of here!"
    B) "Get off that pool table," shouted the bartender the next morning. "Get out of here and don't come back!"
    C) "Get off that pool table! Get out of here and don't come back," shouted the bartender the next morning.
    D) The next morning the bartender shouted, "Get off that pool table! Get out of here and don't come back!"

48) Which of the following examples illustrates a fragment, run-on (or fused) sentence, or comma splice?
    A) Starting easily and purring like a kitten, a Cadillac with a new battery.
    B) Having a new battery, the Cadillac started easily and purred like a kitten.
    C) The Cadillac had a new battery; it started easily and purred like a kitten.
    D) Whenever it had a new battery, the Cadillac started easily and purred like a kitten.

49) Which of the following examples illustrates a fragment, run-on (or fused) sentence, or comma splice?
    A) The whole band laughed when they heard that the bartender's car wouldn't start.
    B) When the band heard that the bartender's car wouldn't start, they all laughed.
    C) News came that the bartender's car wouldn't start; the whole band laughed.
    D) The bartender's car not starting, and the whole band laughing.

50) Which of the following examples illustrates a fragment, run-on (or fused) sentence, or comma splice?
    A) The band drove off into the sunset; the bartender wondered where Elwood had procured a new battery.
    B) As the band drove off into the sunset, the bartender wondered where Elwood had procured a new battery.
    C) The band drove off into the sunset; meanwhile, the bartender wondered where Elwood had procured a new battery.
    D) The band drove off into the sunset, the bartender wondered where Elwood had procured a new battery.

DIAGNOSTIC TEST C

MULTIPLE CHOICE. Choose the one alternative that best completes the statement or answers the question.

1) That is the _____ movie I've ever seen.
    A) worse   B) worst   C) worest   D) most worst

2) Neither of the students _____ on the honor roll.
    A) is   B) are

3) The skier was zooming out of control toward _____.
    A) Suzie and I   B) Suzie and me
    C) we girls   D) them girls

4) I don't have _____ more to say about that.
    A) nothing   B) anything   C) no

5) The limping grizzly bear evidently had hurt _____ paw.
    A) its'   B) it's   C) its

6) The possum, as well as the raccoons, _____ a nuisance.
    A) is   B) are

7) She _____ twenty hours before she fell asleep at the wheel.
    A) had drove   B) drove
    C) had driven   D) done drove

8) Yes, _____ were lost in the mountains for three days.
    A) Craig and I   B) me and Craig   C) us guys

9) Everyone on the men's basketball team who has left _____ stinky shoes in the locker room must remove them today or the shoes will be thrown out.
    A) their   B) his

10) The athlete, exhausted from the long race, slept really _____ last night.
    A) good   B) well

11) Are you _____ by your remarks that I am not in good condition?

    A) implying   B) inferring   C) deliberating

12) What sources do you _____ as evidence?

    A) site   B) sight   C) cite

13) If I _____ you were coming, I would have bought some groceries.

    A) knew   B) had known

    C) would have known   D) would of have

14) I would vote for that candidate again _____ of his extramarital affairs.

    A) regardless   B) irregardless

15) I have decided to stand by my _____ and vote for the Libertarian presidential candidate this year.

    A) principles   B) principals

16) I wish I _____ on vacation in Aruba instead of shoveling snow in Buffalo.

    A) was   B) were

17) The author _____ three novels before her most recent one became a best seller.

    A) wrote   B) had wrote   C) had written

18) She is one of the students who _____ passed the exam.

    A) have   B) has

19) Her favorite activities _____ ice skating, skiing, and snowboarding.

    A) are: B) are,

    C) are the following: D) such as:

20) Jill is the only one of the club members who _____ caught a fish.

    A) has   B) have

21) I performed _____ on the test.

    A) bad   B) badly

22) While out on Halloween, he soaped four _____.

    A) peoples' cars   B) people's cars'

    C) people's cars   D) peoples car's

23) You are voting for _____ in the election?

    A) who   B) whom

24) The sergeant ordered the platoon to gather _____ weapons and supplies immediately.

    A) his   B) her   C) its   D) their

25) Shelia knew that she should have picked up _____ toys two hours ago.

    A) them   B) those   C) all them

26) Which sentence is correct, clear, and concise?
    A) She spun around slowly tucking her body in the camel position.
    B) As she spun around, she slowly tucked her body in the camel position.
    C) She spun around tucking her body in the camel position slowly.

27) Which sentence is correct, clear, and concise?
    A) The opportunity for John to receive a promotion was presented by the company.
    B) John was presented with the opportunity for promotion by his company.
    C) The company offered John a promotion.

28) Which sentence is correct, clear, and concise?
    A) To ace college you should like not goof off too much, study a good amount, and keep track of what your doing.
    B) In order to succeed in college, one must study hard, stay organized, and you should manage your time well.
    C) In order to maximize the results of your efforts in college you should study as hard as you know how, stay absolutely organized to a fault, and not waste the valuable time that is allotted to you here on earth.
    D) To succeed in college, a student should study hard, manage time well, and be organized.

29) Which sentence is correct, clear, and concise?
    A) Through the sport of fishing, my daughter has learned the art of being patient, how to identify various species, and becoming independent.
    B) Becoming independent, the art of patience, and how to identify various species are some of the things which my daughter has learned through the sport of fishing.
    C) Through fishing, my daughter has learned patience, independence, and species identification.
    D) Through fishing, my daughter has learned to be patient, independence, and she's even learned to identify various species.

41

30) Which sentence is correct, clear, and concise?
   A) My favorite bovine buddy Gertrude has ceased to provide the large quantities of milk to which our family has become accustomed.
   B) Gertrude, our cow, has done stopped cranking out the bodacious amounts of milk like we is used to.
   C) Our cow Gertrude's milk production has fallen off precipitously for reasons unknown to farmer or veterinarian's specialist alike in the recent past.
   D) Our cow Gertrude is not giving much milk lately.

31) Which sentence is correct, clear, and concise?
   A) In a recent survey it was determined that more people in the United States seemed to attend pro hockey games now than ten years ago.
   B) Professional hockey game attendance has increased in the United States in the last ten years.
   C) According to a number of measures, there was clear evidence that more fans are going to professional hockey games now than they did ten years ago.
   D) A bunch more people are going to view live hockey games in person than ten years ago.

32) Which sentence is correct, clear, and concise?
   A) It is of paramount importance because of economic uncertainty that the stability of Social Security be enhanced through the intervention of Congress.
   B) In the present climate of economic uncertainty for our valued senior citizens, the lifeblood of their existence—namely Social Security—must be preserved at all costs.
   C) It is vital that Congress protect Social Security.
   D) Social Security, the legacy of FDR and the bulwark of retirement in this day and age for millions of needy Americans, must be protected by Congress in a speedy and timely manner.

33) Which sentence is correct, clear, and concise?
   A) Driving into a ditch while not paying attention because of his mother's cell phone use, the infant was injured.
   B) Driving into a ditch, the infant was injured because his mother was using her car cell phone and not paying attention.
   C) The infant was injured when driving the automobile into a ditch because of his mother's obsessive use of her cell phone.
   D) After driving into a ditch while fumbling with her cell phone, the mother realized that her carelessness had resulted in her infant's injury.

34) Which sentence is correct, clear, and concise?
- A) Some lawyers are known for their lack of ethics.
- B) Some lawyers is known for their lack of ethics.
- C) Every lawyer is known for their lack of ethics.
- D) Every lawyers are known for their lack of ethics.

35) Which sentence is correct, clear, and concise?
- A) The children learned to discriminate among the snakes that are poisonous and the ones that don't have poison.
- B) The children, who learned to discriminate among the snakes that are poisonous, from those that are not.
- C) The children learned to discriminate among the snakes that are poisonous and those that are not.
- D) The children, who learned to discriminate among, the snakes that are poisonous and those that are not.

36) Which sentence best expresses the relationship between the two clauses?
- A) Nancy refuses to eat meat; **therefore**, she consumes nuts, fruits, and tofu.
- B) Nancy refuses to eat meat; **however**, she consumes nuts, fruits, and tofu.
- C) Nancy refuses to eat meat; **in addition**, she consumes nuts, fruits, and tofu.

37) Which sentence best expresses the relationship between the two clauses?
- A) Neil works eighty hours a week; **therefore**, he can't pay his bills.
- B) Neil works eighty hours a week; **consequently**, he can't pay his bills.
- C) Neil works eighty hours a week; **nonetheless**, he can't pay his bills.
- D) Neil works eighty hours a week; **furthermore**, he can't pay his bills.

One of the four underlined sections may mark an error in punctuation. Choose the letter that marks the error in punctuation. If there is no error, choose E.

38) Not <u>surprisingly, people</u> are often naive in choosing careers. <u>People, who</u>
              A   B
want to be police officers often expect glory, excitement, and appreciation.

<u>Oftentimes,</u> the reality is just the opposite. In fact, the work is frequently
    C
characterized by tedious routine, <u>alienation, and</u> a lack of acknowledgement.
                                               D
<u>No error.</u>
   E

39) Here is an interesting <u>anecdote. A</u> wife became increasingly annoyed with her
                                       A

<u>husband's</u> inability or refusal to simply place his dirty socks in a hamper instead
  B

of leaving them strewn all over the floor. Finally she decided she had had enough.

The next time she cleaned the <u>house, she</u> vacuumed up the socks on the <u>floor, and</u>
                                         C   D

continued this strategy until the husband eventually ran out of socks. <u>No error.</u>
                                                                              E

40) When his sock drawer was <u>empty, he</u> asked where all his socks were. His wife
                                          A

said, "They're in the vacuum <u>cleaner: help</u> <u>yourself." After</u> this incident he never
  B   C   D

left socks on the floor again. <u>No error.</u>
                               E

One of the four underlined words in this passage may mark an error in capitalization.
Choose the letter that marks the error. If there is no error, choose E.

41) We had a wonderful visit to the New Orleans area. We ate crawdads at a Bourbon

<u>Street</u> <u>restaurant</u>. We canoed the Mississippi <u>River</u> and were almost run over by a
  A   B   C

barge. We paddled around the Atchafalaya <u>swamp</u> probing for alligators. <u>No error.</u>
                                               D   E

42) William Carlos Williams was a famous <u>American</u> poet, but he was also a <u>doctor.</u>
                                           A   B

Wallace Stevens worked for an insurance company in Hartford, Connecticut.

T. S. Eliot was a <u>banker</u>. Robert Frost was one of the few people who could support
                        C

himself solely on poetry. Many serious poets sustain themselves today by

affiliating with a <u>university.</u> <u>No error.</u>
                    D   E

43) Which of the following examples illustrates a fragment, run-on (or fused) sentence, or comma splice?

    A) The degrees of thinking aloud.   B) Go fish.
    C) Scoot, cat!   D) When visiting a lawyer, bring money.

44) Which of the following examples illustrates a fragment, run-on (or fused) sentence, or comma splice?

    A) I enjoy studying grammar; it is exciting.
    B) What could be more exciting than studying grammar?
    C) I enjoy studying grammar it is exciting.
    D) For excitement, you can't beat grammar.

45) Which of the following examples illustrates a fragment, run-on (or fused) sentence, or comma splice?

    A) There is a surprising ally against winter depression-wind chimes.
    B) Winter depression can be alleviated by wind chimes.
    C) The cheerful sounds of wind chimes can alleviate winter depression.
    D) Wind chimes make cheerful sounds. Which can alleviate winter depression.

46) Which of the following examples illustrates a fragment, run-on (or fused) sentence, or comma splice?

    A) We drove twenty hours straight, then we stayed at a motel.
    B) We drove twenty hours before we stayed at a motel.
    C) After driving twenty hours, we stayed at a motel.
    D) We drove twenty hours, and then we stayed at a motel.

47) Which of the following examples illustrates a fragment, run-on (or fused) sentence, or comma splice?

    A) Teachers appreciate students who accept responsibility for their actions because it demonstrates maturity.
    B) Teachers appreciate students' acceptance of responsibility, for it demonstrates maturity.
    C) Teachers appreciate students who take responsibility for their actions it demonstrates maturity.
    D) Teachers appreciate students who exhibit maturity by taking responsibility for their actions.

48) Which of the following examples illustrates a fragment, run-on (or fused) sentence, or comma splice?
   A) When she went to the emergency room, the doctor looked at her infected hand and gave her antibiotics.
   B) She went to the emergency room because of her infected hand, the doctor gave her antibiotics.
   C) She went to the emergency room and got antibiotics.
   D) She had an infected hand, so she went to the emergency room where a doctor prescribed antibiotics.

49) Which of the following examples illustrates a fragment, run-on (or fused) sentence, or comma splice?
   A) The retired boxer has been selling cars for ten years.
   B) The retired boxer selling cars for ten years.
   C) For ten years the retired boxer has been selling cars.
   D) The boxer has been retired for ten years; now he's selling cars.

50) Which of the following examples illustrates a fragment, run-on (or fused) sentence, or comma splice?
   A) Every presidential election is the same for me; I hold my nose and vote.
   B) I hold my nose and vote in every presidential election.
   C) During every presidential election I hold my nose and vote.
   D) Every presidential election is the same for me, I hold my nose and vote.

DIAGNOSTIC TEST D

MULTIPLE CHOICE. Choose the one alternative that best completes the statement or answers the question.

1) In a department full of rigid thinkers, it is always difficult to _____ any changes.

      A) affect   B) effect

2) The players were at fault for the fighting, but the officials handled the situation _____.

      A) bad   B) badly

3) _____ going to be upset if the puppy you pick is that ugly boxer.

      A) Their   B) There   C) They're

4) _____ is nothing more boring than fishing.

      A) Their   B) There   C) They're

5) Joe is the student _____ lunch box was stuffed with candy.

      A) who's   B) whose

6) Max's Bar is the only establishment in town that offers an interesting bill of _____.

      A) fair   B) fare

7) _____ never too late to learn something new-like word processing!

      A) Its   B) It's   C) Its'

8) Your new necklace _____ your bracelet very nicely.

      A) complements   B) compliments

9) He might be helpful if only he _____ able to use a computer.

      A) was   B) were

10) Neither the driver nor the mechanics on the pit crew _____ what is wrong with the race car.

      A) know   B) knows

11) Any student who wants to succeed must develop _____ computer skills.
    A) his or her B) their

12) The tired child hurriedly _____ his dinner.
    A) ate   B) had ate   C) eat

13) The car pulled in, pulled out, and _____ away from the parking lot.
    A) speeded B) sped   C) speeds

14) The student studied, slept enough hours, and _____ a good breakfast.
    A) had   B) have had C) has   D) having

15) John should learn the _____ before he joins the league.
    A) games rules   B) game's rules
    C) games' rules'   D) game's rule's

16) Seeing your roommate from college twenty years later is frightening, entertaining _____.
    A) and memorable B) , and memorable   C) , and, memorable

17) The old man likes to fish, to hunt, and _____.
    A) swimming   B) to swim C) swim   D) swims

18) I know _____ you met last summer.
    A) who   B) whom

19) _____ late again!
    A) Your   B) You're

20) I can't _____ to see her leave.
    A) bear   B) bare

21) Most prescription drugs have side _____.
    A) affects B) effects

22) My grandfather likes hunting, fishing, and _____
    A) trapping B) trap   C) to trap   D) traps

23) I'd like a _____ worth of gas.
    A) dollars   B) dollar's   C) dollars'

24) He feels _____ about the accident.
    A) bad   B) badly

25) If you want to sleep soundly, you have to _____ down.
    A) lie   B) lay

26) Which sentence is correct, clear, and concise?
    A) Their voting in the election was as important as your's.
    B) Them voting in the election was as important as your's.
    C) Their voting in the election was as important as yours.
    D) Their voting in the election was as important as your's is.

27) Which sentence is correct, clear, and concise?
    A) In spite of all the money they spent on fancy costumes, neither Mary or Beth was a prize winner at the Halloween party.
    B) In spite of all the money they spent on fancy costumes, neither Mary or Beth were a prize winner at the Halloween party.
    C) In spite of all the money they spent on fancy costumes, neither Mary nor Beth were a prize winner at the Halloween party.
    D) In spite of all the money they spent on fancy costumes, neither Mary nor Beth was a prize winner at the Halloween party.

28) Which sentence is correct, clear, and concise?
    A) Our teacher, Mr. Johnson, said "that he had once failed English."
    B) Our teacher, Mr. Johnson, said, "that he had once failed English."
    C) Our teacher, Mr. Johnson, said that he had once failed English.
    D) Our teacher, Mr. Johnson, said, that he had once failed English.

29) Which sentence is correct, clear, and concise?
    A) The following people were elected as officers-Betsy Banes, president, Bill Bates, vice-president; and Fred Farber, treasurer.
    B) The following people were elected as officers: Betsy Banes, president, Bill Bates, vice-president, and Fred Farber, treasurer.
    C) The following people were elected as officers: Betsy Banes, president; Bill Bates, vice-president; and Fred Farber, treasurer.
    D) The following people were elected as officers; Betsy Banes, president; Bill Bates, vice-president; and Fred Farber, treasurer.

30) Which sentence is correct, clear, and concise?
    A) I am excited about attending college, I enjoy learning.
    B) I am excited about attending college, for I enjoy learning.
    C) I am excited about attending college, but I enjoy learning.
    D) I am excited about attending college; because I enjoy learning.

31) Which sentence is correct, clear, and concise?
    A) Although I could never understand his preference for ballet.
    B) Although, I was unable to ever understand his preference for ballet.
    C) Although his preference for ballet was never understandable to me.
    D) However, I could never understand his preference for ballet.

32) Which sentence is correct, clear, and concise?
    A) Leaping over low fences and shallow ditches, the noise of the bull's hooves thundering on the rough ground behind her alarmed Sherry.
    B) Leaping over low fences and shallow ditches, an alarmed Sherry heard the bull's hooves thundering on the rough ground behind her.
    C) Leaping over low fences and shallow ditches, the noise the bull's hooves thundering on the ground behind her was heard by Sherry.
    D) Leaping over low fences and shallow ditches, the bull's hooves thundered on the rough ground alarming Sherry.

33) Which sentence is correct, clear, and concise?
    A) Laying helplessly on its back, the beetle kicked at the air.
    B) The beetle, helplessly lying on its back, kicking at the air.
    C) On its back the beetle laid helplessly and kicked at the air.
    D) Lying helplessly on its back, the beetle kicked at the air.

34) Which sentence is correct, clear, and concise?
    A) The ship builders had to replace the old wooden decks with new decks that were decaying.
    B) With new decks the old wooden decks that were decaying were replaced by the contractors.
    C) The contractors had to replace the decaying wooden decks with new ones.
    D) The wooden decks were decaying; the ship builders had to replace them with new ones.

35) Which sentence is correct, clear, and concise?
  A) People who live in retirement communities are praising not only its cost but also advocating its future growth.
  B) People, who live in retirement communities, are praising not only their cost but also advocating their future growth.
  C) People who live in retirement communities are not only praising its cost but also praising its future growth.
  D) People who live in retirement communities are not only praising their cost but also their future growth.

36) Which sentence best expresses the relationship between the two clauses?
  A) Going to Six Flags was exciting, **but** I think going to Disneyland will be even more adventurous.
  B) Going to Six Flags was exciting; **moreover**, I think going to Disneyland will be even more adventurous.
  C) Going to Six Flags was exciting; **otherwise**, I think going to Disneyland will be even more adventurous.
  D) Going to Six Flags was exciting, **since** I think going to Disneyland will be even more adventurous.

37) Which sentence best expresses the relationship between the two clauses?
  A) The actor had only one goal in life, **yet** he wanted only fame.
  B) The actor had only one goal in life **since** he wanted only fame.
  C) The actor had only one goal in life; **indeed**, he wanted only fame.
  D) The actor had only one goal in life; **however**, he wanted only fame.

Answer: C
Topic: Compound Sentences, Adverbial Conjunctions
References: LB19a, LH35c&52, SFW10&32f, SFH14a, WH54a, NCH48b, DK505

One of the four underlined sections may mark an error in punctuation. Choose the letter that marks the error in punctuation. If there is no error, choose E.

38) The couple shared a love for good books, unusual restaurants, dancing, and hard

work, however, they both had hot tempers and strong wills. Thus, they fought
   A   B   C

often. They are learning to think before they speak and to consider each other's
                                           D

feelings more carefully. No error.
                    E

39) Santa Fe and <u>Taos, which</u> are within an hour's drive of each other, are both cultural
                A

<u>centers: literature,</u> crafts, opera, and art flourish there. For <u>instance, Georgia</u>
  B   C

O'Keefe, the most famous woman artist of this <u>century, lived</u> outside Santa Fe for
                                            D

over the last forty years of her life. <u>No errors.</u>
                                  E

40) Partings are common in life and signal both beginnings and <u>endings. Especially</u> for
                                          A

college freshman and their <u>parents who</u> must say good-bye. They pack clothes,
                        B

books, <u>stereo, and</u> other paraphernalia into their car. They drive off to a college
       C

<u>campus where</u> they enact both an ending and a beginning. <u>No error.</u>
      D   E

One of the four underlined words in this passage may mark an error in capitalization.
Choose the letter that marks the error in capitalization. If there is no error, write E.

41) The <u>Smithsonian</u> <u>Institution</u>, located in Washington, DC, was named after James
      A   B

Smithson, an <u>English</u> <u>Scientist</u>, whose entire estate was left to the United States.
              C   D

<u>No error.</u>
  E

42) Known as the <u>Castle</u>, the Smithsonian was built in a style that architects of that
              A

time referred to as <u>Norman</u>, though today it is usually called <u>Romanesque</u> <u>Revival</u>.
              B   C   D

<u>No error.</u>
  E

43) Which of the following examples illustrates a fragment, run-on (or fused) sentence,
or comma splice?
     A) Fire!
     B) He left town. Without giving me his address.
     C) Get lost!
     D) Jim slammed down the receiver, cutting off our phone conversation.

44) Which of the following examples illustrates a fragment, run-on (or fused) sentence, or comma splice?
- A) When the phone rings. My dog barks excitedly.
- B) I lost the watch that my mother gave me.
- C) He spends every Saturday night in town hanging around bars.
- D) I know that is a sure bet, but I am not a betting person.

45) Which of the following examples illustrates a fragment, run-on (or fused) sentence, or comma splice?
- A) Get a life!
- B) Mary Martin is probably best known for her role in *Peter Pan*.
- C) What a day!
- D) I am usually tired I work the night shift at a service station.

46) Which of the following examples illustrates a fragment, run-on (or fused) sentence, or comma splice?
- A) Because he is trying to control his weight, Jim runs 20 miles a week.
- B) Every summer Tom goes to the mountains, where he hunts small game.
- C) I like to sleep late on Saturday, it is the only day I do not have to work.
- D) The fire was so intense that four companies were called to the blaze.

47) Which of the following examples illustrates a fragment, run-on (or fused) sentence, or comma splice?
- A) He likes swimming, it is good aerobic exercise.
- B) Baseball, the all-American sport, is also played in Japan.
- C) After cutting the grass, Jim was too tired to go dancing.
- D) Please return these library books; they are overdue.

48) Which of the following examples illustrates a fragment, run-on (or fused) sentence, or comma splice?
- A) I do not pay my bills until they are due.
- B) Bob can't drive his car. Until he has the brakes repaired.
- C) When you see Mary, give her my regards.
- D) Please leave now.

49) Which of the following examples illustrates a fragment, run-on (or fused) sentence, or comma splice?
- A) Did you see where I left my keys?
- B) After he parked the car at the far end of the parking lot.
- C) They like to go to the mall, but they socialize rather than shop.
- D) He will telephone me after he arrives at the hotel.

50) Which of the following examples illustrates a fragment, run-on (or fused) sentence, or comma splice?
- A) I know where you went last night.
- B) While you are in town, please do the grocery shopping.
- C) Sue misplaced the gifts that she had bought for Christmas.
- D) The oil slick coated the gulls with a sticky ooze, it would not wash off.

DIAGNOSTIC TEST E

MULTIPLE CHOICE. Choose the one alternative that best completes the statement or answers the question.

1) The unruly students were sent to the office to see the school _____.
   A) principal   B) principle

2) If we don't soon get started, we'll never get _____.
   A) their   B) there   C) they're

3) We had a bad thunderstorm, but the computer system was not _____.
   A) affected   B) effected

4) Each team must elect _____ own captain.
   A) its   B) it's   C) its'

5) I feel _____ about his death.
   A) bad   B) badly

6) _____ often have dinner together.
   A) Me and him   B) Him and me
   C) Him and I   D) He and I

7) Didn't you know what you _____ doing?
   A) were   B) where   C) we're

8) I'm glad _____ back.
   A) you   B) you're

9) Do you think _____ right?
   A) their   B) there   C) they're

10) Are Jim and _____ working on the project together?
    A) she   B) her

11) _____ do you want to see?
    A) Who   B) Whom

12) Did you graduate from _____?
   A) high school   B) High School

13) Brad had his _____.
   A) fathers eyes'   B) father's eyes   C) fathers' eyes

14) I wish he _____ when we asked him to.
   A) would of gone   B) would of went   C) had gone

15) He is the only one of my friends who _____ stayed by me.
   A) have   B) has

16) What are the _____ points of the speech?
   A) principal   B) principle

17) Each of my brothers _____ graduated from college.
   A) have   B) has

18) There are _____ than ten minutes on the parking meter.
   A) less   B) fewer

19) My professor _____ that I would fail the course.
   A) implied   B) inferred

20) Tim is one of my friends who _____ still in high school.
   A) is   B) are

21) The guests _____ Myra, Ted, and Phyllis.
   A) are   B) are: C) are,   D) are;

22) Let's invite the _____ to dinner.
   A) Smiths   B) Smith's   C) Smiths'

23) The plane _____ left before I arrived at the airport.
   A) has   B) have   C) had

24) Please do the _____ go to the baggage area to claim your luggage.
   A) following   B) following,
   C) following;   D) following:

25) I cannot walk any _____.
   A) farther   B) further

26) Which sentence is correct, clear, and concise?
   A) His whining is less annoying than your's is.
   B) His whining is less annoying than yours'.
   C) His whining is less annoying than yours.
   D) His whining is less annoying than your's.

27) Which sentence is correct, clear, and concise?
   A) Despite months of planning and training, neither Hans nor Lars were able to reach the summit of Mt. Everest.
   B) Despite months of planning and training, neither Hans or Lars was able to reach the summit of Mt. Everest.
   C) Despite months of planning and training, neither Hans or Lars were able to reach the summit of Mt. Everest.
   D) Despite months of planning and training, neither Hans nor Lars was able to reach the summit of Mt. Everest.

28) Which sentence is correct, clear, and concise?
   A) Mrs. Bland, our drama coach, said that our performance was very inspiring.
   B) Mrs. Bland, our drama coach, said "that our performance was very inspiring."
   C) Mrs. Bland our drama coach said that our performance was very inspiring.
   D) Mrs. Bland our drama coach said "that our performance was very inspiring."

29) Which sentence is correct, clear, and concise?
   A) When I see that big smile spread across his face.
   B) Then, when I see that big smile spread across his face.
   C) And when I see that big smile spread across his face.
   D) When I see that big smile spread across his face, I smile back!

30) Which sentence is correct, clear, and concise?
   A) I have owned the following pets; Fanny, a goldfish, Lord Fairfax, an English bulldog, Squeaky, a gerbil, and Prissy, a cat.
   B) I have owned the following pets; Fanny, a goldfish; Lord Fairfax, an English bulldog; Squeaky, a gerbil; and Prissy, a cat.
   C) I have owned the following pets-Fanny, a goldfish; Lord Fairfax, an English bulldog; Squeaky, a gerbil; and Prissy, a cat.
   D) I have owned the following pets: Fanny, a goldfish; Lord Fairfax, an English bulldog; Squeaky, a gerbil; and Prissy, a cat.

31) Which sentence is correct, clear, and concise?
   A) The sensible young woman decided to stop speaking to her neighbor, for she could not hardly speak to him without getting into a heated argument.
   B) The sensible young woman decided to stop speaking to her neighbor for she could not hardly speak to him without getting into a heated argument.
   C) The sensible young woman decided to stop speaking to her neighbor, for she could hardly speak to him without getting into a heated argument.

32) Which sentence is correct, clear, and concise?
   A) Every man, woman, and child who watch Westerns knows that pork and beans are a cowboy's favorite meal.
   B) Every man, woman, and child who watches Westerns knows that pork and beans is a cowboy's favorite meal.
   C) Every man, woman, and child, who watch Westerns, knows that pork and beans is a cowboy's favorite meal.
   D) Every man, woman, and child who watches Westerns knows that pork and beans are a cowboy's favorite meal.

33) Which sentence is correct, clear, and concise?
   A) "I will always think of him," the wizened old woman said "as a colossal fool and a braggart."
   B) "I will always think of him," the wizened old woman said, "as a colossal fool and a braggart."
   C) "I will always think of him," the wizened old woman said, "As a colossal fool and a braggart."

58

34) Which sentence is correct, clear, and concise?
   A) I enjoy going to Little League games because the parents are fun to watch, the children's enthusiasm, and seeing the children improve.
   B) I enjoy going to Little League games with the parents are fun to watch and the children getting excited and better at their sport.
   C) I enjoy going to Little League games because the parents are fun to watch, the children are humorous to see, and the young athletes' improvement is exciting to witness.
   D) I enjoy going to Little League games especially the parents, the children, and the progress.

35) Which sentence is correct, clear, and concise?
   A) Singing in the chorus, acting in the class play, band playing, Jack devoted little time to studying.
   B) Jack devoted-singing in the chorus, acting in the class play, band playing-little time to studying.
   C) Singing in the chorus, acting in the class play, and playing in the band, Jack devoted little time to studying.
   D) Singing in the chorus, acting in the class play, band playing, Jack devoted little time in studying.

36) Which sentence best expresses the relationship between the two clauses?
   A) His father told him typing was women's work; **however**, he developed no keyboard skills and can't use a computer.
   B) His father told him typing was women's work; **nevertheless**, he developed no keyboard skills and can't use a computer.
   C) His father told him typing was women's work; **consequently**, he developed no keyboard skills and can't use a computer.
   D) His father told him typing was women's work; **on the contrary**, he developed no keyboard skills and can't use a computer.

37) Which sentence best expresses the relationship between the two clauses?
   A) College students drive old, unreliable cars; **as a result**, they still make it to Florida for spring break.
   B) College students drive old, unreliable cars; **indeed**, they still make it to Florida for spring break.
   C) College students drive old, unreliable cars; **therefore**, they still make it to Florida for spring break.
   D) College students drive old, unreliable cars; **nevertheless**, they still make it to Florida for spring break.

One of the four underlined sections may mark an error in punctuation. Choose the letter that marks the error in punctuation. If there is no error, choose E.

38) <u>Graceland, located</u> in Memphis, <u>Tennessee, is</u> the estate of the late Elvis
        A   B

<u>Presley, the</u> hip-<u>gyrating, king</u> of rock and roll. <u>No error.</u>
   C   D   E

39) Now a <u>museum, Graceland</u> is dedicated to the memory of <u>Elvis, and</u> the
           A   B

perpetuation of Elvis mania. Adoring fans crowd the <u>grounds, hoping</u> to catch a
                                                       C

glimpse of the <u>King, whose</u> music is still popular today. <u>No error.</u>
              D   E

40) Elvis combined the sounds of popular, country, and gospel <u>music, as</u> well as
                                                         A

rhythm and <u>blues, into</u> his own unique <u>sound, and</u> by the late 1950's he was an
           B   C

international sensation. His music blurred the social and racial barriers of that

<u>era, ushering</u> in a new musical and popular culture. <u>No error.</u>
  D   E

One of the four underlined words in this passage may mark an error in capitalization. Choose the letter that marks the error in capitalization. If there is no error, write E.

41) In the early 19th <u>century,</u> <u>Neoclassical</u> architecture flourished throughout the
                          A   B

United States. Modeled after <u>Roman</u> and, later, <u>Greek</u> architecture, this style was
                             C   D

intended to reflect the political ideals as well as the architectural style of that era.

<u>No error.</u>
  E

42) Thomas Jefferson, the third <u>President,</u> modeled the Virginia <u>State</u> <u>Capitol</u> on an
                              A   B   C

ancient Roman temple. His own house at <u>Monticello</u> was inspired by the design of
                                     D

an ancient Roman villa. <u>No error.</u>
                     E

43) Which of the following examples illustrates a fragment, run-on (or fused) sentence, or comma splice?
   A) Please lend me a pen I lost mine.
   B) I missed my ride today because I overslept.
   C) Let's take a walk.
   D) Scram!

44) Which of the following examples illustrates a fragment, run-on (or fused) sentence, or comma splice?
   A) Let's go to the game next Friday.
   B) As I pulled into the parking lot near the vacant lot.
   C) After his retirement, he moved to the suburbs.
   D) My birthday is Saturday, not Sunday.

45) Which of the following examples illustrates a fragment, run-on (or fused) sentence, or comma splice?
   A) He never tells the truth unless he has to.
   B) I won't dance don't ask me.
   C) Get out!
   D) After he washes the dishes, he scrubs the floor.

46) Which of the following examples illustrates a fragment, run-on (or fused) sentence, or comma splice?
   A) Announcing the arrival of spring, the crocus is the first flower to bloom.
   B) Have you paid all the bills that are overdue?
   C) The phone is ringing, please answer it.
   D) Every Sunday afternoon, we took a long leisurely walk.

47) Which of the following examples illustrates a fragment, run-on (or fused) sentence, or comma splice?
   A) Having dressed in my best suit for the long-awaited interview.
   B) Shall we go to the movies tonight?
   C) Bring in the clowns.
   D) When you are ready, please phone me.

48) Which of the following examples illustrates a fragment, run-on (or fused) sentence, or comma splice?
   A) Do you like the tango, or do you prefer the fox trot?
   B) Steinbeck liked to write about the working class and down-and-out characters.
   C) I lost, but I don't care.
   D) As the hail pelted the car, leaving deep dents in the hood.

49) Which of the following examples illustrates a fragment, run-on (or fused) sentence, or comma splice?
- A) Surprisingly, college is not all hard work.
- B) When the movie is shown again, let's go.
- C) The towhee, sometimes called a robin.
- D) Protest without constructive criticism is of little value.

50) Which of the following examples illustrates a fragment, run-on (or fused) sentence, or comma splice?
- A) Becky was nervous and depressed she was overworked.
- B) Aware of his social blunder, Kevin was quick to apologize.
- C) I closed my eyes, drifting off into a sound sleep.
- D) After gardening, he was too tired and sore to go out.

DIAGNOSTIC TEST F

MULTIPLE CHOICE. Choose the one alternative that best completes the statement or answers the question.

1) My little brother is taller than _____.
   A) I   B) me

2) To avoid a penalty _____ important to pay taxes on time.
   A) its   B) it's   C) its'

3) I graduated from _____.
   A) High school   B) High School
   C) Central High School   D) Central high school

4) Little children like to pull their _____.
   A) cat's tails B) cats tail's C) cats tails' D) cats' tails

5) Please list the _____ points of your research.
   A) principal   B) principle

6) I would not have failed the test if I _____ followed the instructions.
   A) would of   B) would have   C) had

7) She cried for two days because her dog _____.
   A) have died   B) has died   C) had died

8) _____ are going on a field trip.
   A) Him and I   B) He and I   C) Him and me

9) He is the only one of my friends who _____ offered constant support.
   A) has   B) have

10) His stern lecture _____ that I would not pass the course.
    A) implied   B) inferred

11) Are you aware of the _____ of combining drugs?
    A) affects   B) effects

12) His address is as _____ 100 South Main Street.
    A) follows   B) follows: C) follows;   D) follows,

13) The television programs that I dislike the most _____ those with violence.
    A) are: B) are;   C) are,   D) are

14) I don't know what they _____ doing last night.
    A) were   B) where   C) we're

15) The team has to submit _____ schedule for the next season.
    A) his   B) her   C) his or her   D) their

16) I don't know _____ he has finished the report.
    A) weather   B) whether

17) Do you know if _____ going with us?
    A) they're   B) their   C) there

18) I really do not care for _____ singing.
    A) him   B) his

19) The train _____ before I arrived at the station.
    A) has left   B) had left   C) left

20) Hungary is one of the small European countries that _____ a history of political oppression.
    A) have   B) has

21) He _____ swallow his food.
    A) could hardly   B) couldn't hardly

22) The meeting lost _____ focus.
    A) its   B) it's   C) its'

23) Neither her brother nor her sister _____ offered to help her.
    A) have   B) has

24) This restaurant is definitely the _____ of the two.

    A) best   B) better

25) Do you know what _____ going to do tonight?

    A) your   B) you're   C) youre

26) Which sentence is correct, clear, and concise?
    A) The boy, whom everyone thought was least likely to succeed, became wealthy.
    B) The boy, who everyone thought was least likely to succeed, became surprisingly wealthy.
    C) The boy whose least likely to succeed, everyone thought, became surprisingly wealthy.
    D) The boy, whom everyone thought, was least likely to succeed became surprisingly wealthy.

27) Which sentence is correct, clear, and concise?
    A) Redecorating her room, listening to rock music, and harp practicing, Sarah reveled in her spring break.
    B) Redecorating her room, listening to rock music, and harp practicing, Sarah reveled in her Spring break.
    C) Redecorating her room, listening to rock music, and practicing the harp, Sarah reveled in her spring break.

28) Which sentence is correct, clear, and concise?
    A) When leaving the hotel check for belongings, lights turned out, and return your key to the registration desk.
    B) When leaving the hotel, checking for belongings, turning lights out, and returning your key to the registration desk.
    C) When departing and checking out of the hotel, it is necessary for you to always check for belongings, turn out lights, and return your key to the registration desk.
    D) Check for belongings, turn out lights, and return your key to the registration desk when leaving the hotel.

29) Which sentence is correct, clear, and concise?
   A) The only hope, according to one farmer, is a year of good weather and high prices.
   B) The only hope according to one farmer is a year of good weather and high prices.
   C) The only hope, according to one farmer, are a year of good weather and high prices.
   D) The only hope according to one farmer are a year of good weather and high prices.

30) Which sentence is correct, clear, and concise?
   A) Judy was obviously in pain, her ankle having been broken in the fall.
   B) Judy was obviously in pain; her ankle having been broken in the fall.
   C) Judy was obviously in pain, her ankle having been broken, in the fall.

31) Which sentence is correct, clear, and concise?
   A) Aerobics classes at the YMCA had to be scheduled around classes in wood carving, quilt making, and how to paint landscapes.
   B) Aerobics classes at the YMCA had to be scheduled around classes in how to carve wood, how to make a quilt, and how to paint landscapes.
   C) Aerobics classes at the YMCA had to be scheduled around classes in wood carving, quilt making, and landscape painting.

32) Which sentence is correct, clear, and concise?
   A) "This team had better learn to play together," said the manager, if it expects to win."
   B) "This team had better learn to play together," said the manager, "if it expects to win."
   C) "This team had better learn to play together," said the manager, if it expects to win".

33) Which sentence is correct, clear, and concise?
   A) Although he ran a red light does not make him a criminal.
   B) Although he ran a red light that does not make him a criminal.
   C) Although he ran a red light, that does not make him a criminal.
   D) Running a red light does not make him a criminal.

34) Which sentence is correct, clear, and concise?
   A) Tomorrow there will be precipitation in the form of snow shower activity.
   B) Tomorrow's weather activity will be in the form of snow showers.
   C) Tomorrow it will snow.
   D) Tomorrow's weather will be snow shower activity.

35) Which sentence is correct, clear, and concise?
    A) The decision, that of postponing the meeting, was made by them.
    B) The decision to postpone the meeting was made by them.
    C) The decision of postponing the meeting was made by them.
    D) They decided to postpone the meeting.

36) Which sentence best expresses the relationship between the two clauses?
    A) The novel was a critical success; **however**, its sales were disappointing.
    B) The novel was a critical success; **moreover**, its sales were disappointing.
    C) The novel was a critical success; **indeed**, its sales were disappointing.
    D) The novel was a critical success; **therefore**, its sales were disappointing.

37) Which sentence best expresses the relationship between the two clauses?
    A) The newest trend in soft drinks is natural fruit juices; **consequently**, colas still sell more.
    B) The newest trend in soft drinks is natural fruit juices; **otherwise**, colas still sell more.
    C) The newest trend in soft drinks is natural fruit juices; **therefore**, colas still sell more.
    D) The newest trend in soft drinks is natural fruit juices; **however**, colas still sell more.

One of the four underlined sections may mark an error in punctuation. Choose the letter that marks the error in punctuation. If there is no error, choose E.

38) The Berlin <u>Wall, built</u> on August 12, 1961, was erected to prevent the people of
                  A

East Berlin from escaping to West Berlin. The original <u>wall, constructed</u> of barbed
                                                        B

wire and cinder <u>block, was</u> later replaced by a series of <u>high, concrete</u> walls that
                  C   D

were topped with barbed wire and mines. <u>No error</u>.
                                              E

39) Extending about a hundred <u>miles, the</u> Wall separated families and friends. About
                                A

5,000 East Germans managed to cross the <u>Wall, however,</u> and escape to safety in
                                                B

<u>West Berlin; another</u> 5,000 were captured and 190 were killed. The Wall remained
          C

a symbol of the Cold <u>War; separating</u> Eastern Europe from Western Europe, until it
                          D

fell in November 1989. <u>No error</u>.
                    E

40) Genetically engineered <u>food-created</u> by injecting the seed of one crop with a gene
                                    A

from another <u>organism, to</u> make the crop more resistant to disease, <u>drought, or</u>
                    B   C

<u>weeds-is</u> causing a controversy among health-conscious Americans. <u>No error.</u>
  D   E

One of the four underlined words in this passage may mark an error in capitalization.
Choose the letter that marks the error in capitalization. If there is no error, write E.

41) The <u>Vietnam</u> <u>Veterans</u> <u>Memorial</u> was authorized by <u>Congress</u> in 1980. It was
          A   B   C   D

intended as a testament to the veterans who served in one of the United States'

most unpopular wars. <u>No error.</u>
                       E

42) The <u>Wall</u>, listing the names of servicemen who had died, was erected in 1982 in
          A

Washington, D. C., on the <u>National</u> <u>Mall</u>. The <u>Monument</u> has become one of
                               B   C   D

Washington's most popular sites. <u>No error.</u>
                                  E

43) Which of the following examples illustrates a fragment, run-on (or fused) sentence, or comma splice?
    A) Bill liked school, but he was failing history.
    B) Bill liked school although he was failing history.
    C) Bill liked school, he was, however, failing history.
    D) Although Bill liked school, he was failing history.

44) Which of the following examples illustrates a fragment, run-on (or fused) sentence, or comma splice?
    A) Disgusted because he was failing history, Bill refused to leave his room.
    B) Bill was disgusted because he was failing history and refused to leave his room.
    C) Bill, disgusted because he was failing history, refused to leave his room.
    D) Bill, disgusted because he was failing history, and refusing to leave his room.

45) Which of the following examples illustrates a fragment, run-on (or fused) sentence, or comma splice?
    A) Clara was sympathetic because Bill was so cute.
    B) Because Bill was so cute, Clara was sympathetic.
    C) Although Clara was sympathetic because Bill was so cute.
    D) Clara was sympathetic; indeed Bill was really cute.

46) Which of the following examples illustrates a fragment, run-on (or fused) sentence, or comma splice?
    A) "If you fail history," said Bill's father. "You'll go to military school."
    B) "You'll go to military school if you fail history," said Bill's father.
    C) "If you fail history, you'll go to military school," said Bill's father.
    D) Bill's father said, "You'll go to military school if you fail history."

47) Which of the following examples illustrates a fragment, run-on (or fused) sentence, or comma splice?
    A) Bill had poor study habits, for he played video games every evening.
    B) Playing video games every evening, Bill neglected to study.
    C) Bill, having poor study habits and playing video games every evening.
    D) Bill had poor study habits; in fact, he played video games every evening.

48) Which of the following examples illustrates a fragment, run-on (or fused) sentence, or comma splice?
    A) Clara phoned Bill every night, she encouraged him to develop better study habits.
    B) When Clara phoned Bill, she encouraged him to develop better study habits.
    C) Clara phoned Bill every night; she encouraged him, moreover, to develop better study habits.
    D) Every night Clara talked to Bill on the phone; she encouraged him to develop better study habits.

49) Which of the following examples illustrates a fragment, run-on (or fused) sentence, or comma splice?
    A) Bill studied harder; he soon began to earn passing grades.
    B) Bill studied harder, then he began to earn passing grades.
    C) Bill studied harder, so he soon began to earn passing grades.
    D) Bill studied harder; therefore, he soon began to earn passing grades.

50) Which of the following examples illustrates a fragment, run-on (or fused) sentence, or comma splice?
    A) Trying his best to impress Clara, Bill studied even harder.
    B) Bill tried his best to impress Clara by studying even harder.
    C) Because Bill studied harder and tried his best to impress Clara.
    D) Bill tried his best to impress Clara; as a result, he tried even harder.

DIAGNOSTIC TEST G

MULTIPLE CHOICE. Choose the one alternative that best completes the statement or answers the question.

Choose the underlined and lettered selection that is unnecessary within the context of the passage.

1) After <u>much</u> deliberation, we <u>still</u> couldn't decide whether to take a course in the
         A   B
<u>basic</u> fundamentals of algebra or <u>advanced</u> composition.
   C   D

      A) much   B) still   C) basic   D) advanced

2) Regarded as the <u>preeminent</u> novelist of our age, Alexander Solzhenitsyn often
                         A
returned <u>back</u> in his novels to the gulags where he suffered years of <u>forced</u> labor,
         B   C
beatings, and <u>other</u> indignities.
              D

      A) preeminent   B) back   C) forced   D) other

3) Which sentence expresses the intended meaning most clearly and concisely?
      A) The car wouldn't start due to the fact that there was a leak in the fuel line.
      B) The car wouldn't start at all because there was a leak in the fuel line.
      C) The car wouldn't start because there was a leak in the fuel line.
      D) The car wouldn't start because of a leak in the fuel line.

Select the most effective word or phrase within the context of the sentence.

4) Edward tried with all his _____ to lift the fallen beam in order to free the earthquake victim trapped beneath it.
      A) power   B) might   C) force

5) Despite Representative Pendergast's _____ lead in the polls, when the balloting ended, she had lost the election.
      A) narrow   B) skinny   C) thin

6) Global politics makes strange bedfellows: one year a leader condemns his opponent for _____ the people's rights and aspirations; the next year they share the Nobel Prize for Peace.

        A) repressing   B) sublimating   C) suppressing

7) Which sentence is correct, clear, and concise?
    A) Gripping the limestone crevices, the fugitive's eyes strained trying to recognize shapes in the darkness.
    B) Gripping the limestone crevices in the darkness, the fugitive's eyes strained trying to recognize shapes.
    C) Gripping the limestone crevices, the fugitive strained his eyes, trying to recognize shapes in the darkness.
    D) Gripping the limestone crevices trying to recognize shapes, the fugitive strained his eyes in the darkness.

8) Which sentence is correct, clear, and concise?
    A) Many products can be purchased at department stores that require assembly.
    B) Many products at department stores can be purchased that require assembly.
    C) Many products can be purchased that require assembly at department stores.
    D) Many products that require assembly can be purchased at department stores.

9) Which sentence is correct, clear, and concise?
    A) The Thai chef brought out grouper masaman curry, to his special customer smothered in peanuts and potato cubes.
    B) The Thai chef brought out grouper masaman curry, smothered in peanuts and potato cubes, to his special customer.
    C) Smothered in peanuts and potato cubes, the Thai chef brought out grouper masaman curry to his special customer.
    D) To his special customer, the Thai chef brought out, smothered in peanuts and potato cubes, grouper masaman curry.

10) Which sentence is correct, clear, and concise?
    A) We spoke to each other often on the phone, but we saw each other only on rare occasions.
    B) We often spoke to each other on the phone, but we only saw each other on rare occasions.
    C) We spoke to each other on the phone often, but we saw only each other on rare occasions.
    D) We often spoke to each other on the phone, but we saw each other only on rare occasions.

11) Which sentence expresses the meaning with the most fluency and the clearest logic?
   A) There are many communities in South Florida. They have their own golf courses, so the area has become a mecca for golfers.
   B) Many of South Florida's communities have their own golf courses, and the area has become a mecca for golfers.
   C) Because many of South Florida's communities have their own golf courses, the area has become a mecca for golfers.
   D) Because many of South Florida's communities have their own golf courses; therefore, the area has become a mecca for golfers.

12) Which sentence expresses the meaning with the most fluency and the clearest logic?
   A) Writing biographies of historical figures is stimulating, and it also develops research skills.
   B) Writing biographies of historical figures is stimulating while it also develops research skills.
   C) Writing biographies of historical figures is not only stimulating but also develops research skills.
   D) Since writing biographies of historical figures is stimulating, it develops research skills.

13) Which sentence expresses the meaning with the most fluency and the clearest logic?
   A) They had good educations; they also had secure jobs. They decided that evening to get married.
   B) They had good educations, they had secure jobs, and they decided that evening to get married.
   C) They had good educations and secure jobs, so they decided that evening to get married.
   D) They had good educations and secure jobs, and that evening they decided to get married.

14) Which sentence expresses the meaning with the most fluency and the clearest logic?
   A) Some children appear withdrawn in the classroom. They may have learning styles that are different from the teacher's mode of presentation.
   B) Some children who appear withdrawn in the classroom may have learning styles that are different from the teacher's mode of presentation.
   C) Some children appear withdrawn in the classroom, and they may have learning styles that are different from the teacher's mode of presentation.
   D) Some children appear withdrawn in the classroom; therefore, they may have learning styles that are different from the teacher's mode of presentation.

15) Which sentence is correct, clear, and effective?
A) Poor environmental planning will lead to unacceptable levels of soil erosion, intolerable amounts of pesticide use, and a quality of life that will be diminished.
B) Poor environmental planning will lead to unacceptable soil erosion levels, amounts of pesticide use that are intolerable, and a diminished quality of life.
C) Poor environmental planning will lead to unacceptable levels of soil erosion, intolerable amounts of pesticide use, and a diminished quality of life.

16) Which sentence is the most clear and effective?
A) Learning water skiing is very different from learning how to snow ski.
B) Learning to water ski is very different from learning to snow ski.
C) Learning how to water ski is very different from learning snow skiing.
D) To learn to water ski is very different from learning to snow ski.

17) Which sentence is correct, clear, and concise?
A) Janice was an accomplished pianist, played tennis skillfully, and was a gourmet cook.
B) Janice was accomplished on the piano, was a skillful tennis player, and was a gourmet cook.
C) Janice was an accomplished pianist, a skillful tennis player, and a gourmet cook.
D) A gourmet cook, Janice was also an accomplished pianist and a tennis player who was skillful.

Choose the correct option to replace the underlined words.

18) South Florida is known for its fun in the <u>sun it</u> also has a solid reputation as a high-tech manufacturing center.
    A) sun, it   B) sun but, it   C) sun, but it   D) no change

19) Ted walked the entire length of the world's largest shopping <u>mall, after</u> he reached its end, he still couldn't find a pair of sneakers that fit.
    A) mall; after B) mall after   C) mall—after   D) no change

20) Long-distance telephone carriers competing with high-tech <u>options</u>. <u>They have</u> made choosing a telecommunications system even more complicated.
    A) options they have   B) options have
    C) options; they have   D) no change

21) Earning close to $700 a <u>week</u>. <u>She</u> is hardworking, diligent, dedicated, and innovative.
    A) week she   B) week; she   C) week, she   D) no change

74

22) A brilliant scientist with many remarkable achievements in her <u>field. Dr. Farakis</u> is this year's recipient of the Nobel Prize for Biology.

    A) field Dr. Farakis   B) field; Dr. Farakis

    C) field, Dr. Farakis   D) no change

23) My professor and my classmates <u>are</u> engaged in discussions about AIDS, but neither they nor she <u>agree</u> on many issues.

    A) are, agrees   B) is, agree   C) is, agrees   D) no change

24) Each of the students <u>has</u> to give a five-minute speech; in addition, he or she <u>have</u> to use a visual aid.

    A) has, has   B) have, have   C) have, has   D) no change

25) One of the leading economic analysts <u>say</u> that the market for catalog sales <u>is</u> very lucrative today.

    A) say, are   B) says, are   C) says, is   D) no change

26) Expanding to the rainforests and coral reefs, eco-tours <u>appeal</u> to some who <u>seek</u> environmentally sound adventure.

    A) appeals, seeks   B) appeal, seeks   C) appeals, seek   D) no change

27) Between you and <u>I</u> , there isn't one among the three of them <u>who</u> can do the job.

    A) I, whom   B) me, whom   C) me, who   D) no change

28) Dexter and <u>she</u> gave Hank and <u>I</u> a ride to the airport.

    A) she, me   B) her, me   C) her, I   D) no change

29) One of the students turned in <u>her</u> research paper before <u>she</u> should have.

    A) their, they   B) her, they   C) their, she   D) no change

30) During <u>their</u> quarterly meeting, Essex Corporation showed the annual report electronically to <u>their</u> Board members.

    A) their, its   B) its, their   C) its, its   D) no change

31) <u>In the local paper it reported</u> that the funeral would be held at 10:00 a.m. at Forest
Lawn Cemetery.
- A) In the local paper, they reported
- B) The local paper reported
- C) In the local paper, it was reported
- D) no change

Choose the correct option among the answers given.

32) If we <u>accept</u> your <u>advise</u>, we should <u>adopt</u> the new program as is by the first of the
         A   B   C
month.
- A) expect   B) advice   C) adapt   D) no change

33) After reading about the civil war <u>among</u> the two major factions, I was <u>further</u>
                                   A   B
<u>irritated</u> to learn that U.N. efforts to enforce a cease fire had failed.
  C
- A) between   B) farther   C) aggravated   D) no change

34) <u>It's</u> hard not to be <u>effected</u> by the plight of those who <u>immigrate</u> to the United
   A   B   C
States because their lives are in danger.
- A) Its   B) affected   C) emigrate   D) no change

35) Marcel was <u>use</u> to waiting for the bus, so he was not <u>surprise</u> when it was late.
         A   B
- A) used, surprise B) used, surprised C) use, surprised D) no change

36) I could study more effectively if there <u>were</u> fewer distractions.
                                          A
- A) was   B) would be   C) no change

37) After the accident <u>was</u> cleared from the highway, Anne and I were able to continue
on our way.
- A) had been B) were   C) no change

38) Which sentence is most logical and correctly expresses the comparison?
- A) Marco is much smarter than most people think.
- B) Marco is much smarter then most people think.
- C) Marco is much smarter than most people think he is.

39) Which sentence is most logical and correctly expresses the comparison?
   A) Of the two countries, Switzerland and France, Switzerland has the most mountains.
   B) Of the two countries, Switzerland and France, Switzerland has more mountains.
   C) Of the two countries, Switzerland and France, Switzerland is the most mountainous.

40) Which sentence is most logical and correctly expresses the comparison?
   A) In Minnesota, air-conditioned cars are not as necessary as Florida.
   B) In Minnesota, air-conditioned cars are not as necessary as they are in Florida.
   C) In Minnesota, air-conditioned cars are not as necessary as in Florida.

Choose the correct option.

41) Anita's piano was _____ by Mr. Chaffey.
   A) finely tuned   B) fine tuned   C) fine tune

42) We felt <u>badly</u> because the tour had not been running <u>smoothly</u> in spite of all our
          A   B
<u>well-intentioned</u> efforts.
          C
   A) bad   B) smooth   C) well intention   D) no change

Choose the correct option from the answers given.

43) The <u>Mayors</u> of several small cities met with <u>Governor</u> Polk in
          A   B
<u>Spokane, Washington</u>, to discuss urban issues.
          C
   A) mayors   B) governor   C) spokane, washington   D) no change

44) Wilburn and Starke, located on <u>Third Avenue</u>, keeps <u>Summer</u> hours from nine
                                        A   B
o'clock to three until <u>September</u>.
                           C
   A) third avenue   B) summer   C) september   D) no change

45) While I was <u>studying</u> for the exam, an unfortunate incident <u>occured</u>. I <u>accidentally</u>
                    A   B   C
set fire to my notes.
   A) studying   B) occurred   C) accidentally   D) no change

46) <u>Height</u> and weight are two <u>seperate</u> factors; after age twenty-one, one is

    A   B

<u>changeable,</u> the other is not.

    C

      A) Heighth   B) separate   C) changable   D) no change

Choose the correctly punctuated option.

47) The brothers planned to hike to the bottom of the <u>Grand Canyon but,</u> they changed their minds because of the extremely hot weather.

      A) Canyon; but   B) Canyon, but   C) Canyon but   D) no change

48) "Where are the two of you going after <u>work."? he asked?</u>

      A) work?" he asked.   B) work"? he asked

      C) work?", he asked   D) no change

49) Rafting down the Colorado <u>River, one of the fastest in the world,</u> was the high point of our vacation.

      A) River one of the fastest in the world, was

      B) River one of the fastest in the world was

      C) River, one of the fastest in the world was

      D) no change

50) Which sentence is correct, clear, and concise?

      A) Because of the change in weather <u>conditions we</u> decided not to rest before descending the mountain.

      B) Because of the change in weather <u>conditions, we</u> decided not to rest before descending the mountain.

      C) We decided not to descend the <u>mountain, because</u> of the change in weather conditions.

DIAGNOSTIC TEST H

MULTIPLE CHOICE. Choose the one alternative that best completes the statement or answers the question.

Choose the underlined and lettered selection that is unnecessary within the context of the passage.

1) Even though we consulted our <u>high-priced</u> decorator, we still could not select a
   A
color <u>from the chart</u>, but we finally selected <u>the color</u> <u>red</u>.
      B   C   D
        A) high-priced   B) from the chart   C) the color   D) red

2) The <u>tightly</u> coiled rattler waited <u>under the rock</u> to strike its <u>unsuspecting</u> prey with
         A   B   C
its <u>deadly</u> lethal fangs.
    D
        A) tightly   B) under the rock   C) unsuspecting   D) deadly

3) Which sentence is the most clear and concise?
   A) It is a fact that there are many solutions that can be found to the complex environmental issues of today.
   B) There are many solutions that can be found to the complex environmental issues of today.
   C) Many solutions can be found to today's complex environmental issues.
   D) The complex environmental issues of today have many solutions that can be found.

Select the most effective word or phrase within the context of the sentence.

4) Even extra-strength aspirin couldn't _____ my headaches.
       A) heal   B) relieve   C) cure

5) In a quiet, almost hesitant manner, Jane _____ that the charges against her were untrue.
       A) responded   B) exclaimed   C) retorted

6) Joan's superior leadership style is regarded as a(n) _____ of professional mentoring.
       A) pattern   B) illustration   C) model

79

7) Which sentence is correct, clear, and concise?
    A) By working overtime, enough money was saved by John to make a down payment on a new car.
    B) Enough money was saved by John, by working overtime, to make a down payment on a new car.
    C) By working overtime, John saved enough money to make a down payment on a new car.
    D) John saved enough money to make a down payment on a new car by working overtime.

8) Which sentence is correct, clear, and concise?
    A) Formula can be bought at the supermarket already sterilized, which requires minimal preparation.
    B) Already sterilized at the supermarket, formula can be bought which requires minimal preparation.
    C) Already sterilized formula, which requires minimal preparation, can be bought at the supermarket.
    D) Formula, which requires minimal preparation, can be bought at the supermarket, which is already sterilized.

9) Which sentence expresses the meaning with the most fluency and has the clearest logic within the context?
    A) Herbal remedies are growing in popularity, and they account for $87 million in over-the-counter sales nationwide.
    B) Herbal remedies are growing in popularity; however, they account for $87 million in over-the-counter sales nationwide.
    C) Herbal remedies are growing in popularity because they account for $87 million in over-the-counter sales nationwide.
    D) Herbal remedies, which are growing in popularity, account for $87 million in over-the-counter sales nationwide.

10) Which sentence is correct, clear, and concise?
    A) After we exchanged phone numbers, we agreed to call each other at least once a week.
    B) At least once a week, we agreed to call each other after we exchanged phone numbers.
    C) We agreed, after exchanging phone numbers to call each other, at least once a week.
    D) After we exchanged phone numbers, we agreed at least once a week to call each other.

11) Which sentence expresses the meaning with the most fluency and has the clearest logic within the context?

A) Affording quality child care is a concern of single working parents who must arrange for sick days and school holidays.

B) Affording quality child care is a concern of single working parents, they must arrange for sick days and school holidays.

C) Affording quality child care is a concern of single working parents, and they must arrange for sick days and school holidays.

D) Affording quality child care is a concern of single working parents; also arranging for sick days and school holidays.

12) Which sentence expresses the meaning with the most fluency and has the clearest logic within the context?

A) The report addresses community responses to illiteracy. It was written collaboratively.

B) The report that addresses community responses to illiteracy was written collaboratively.

C) The report that addresses community responses to illiteracy and was written collaboratively.

D) The report addresses community responses to illiteracy, as it was written collaboratively.

13) Which sentence expresses the meaning with the most fluency and has the clearest logic within the context?

A) Here are the winning tickets. Their holders live in different regions of the state. They will share the jackpot.

B) The holders of the winning tickets, who will share the jackpot, live in different regions of the state.

C) Although they live in different regions of the state, holders of the winning tickets will share the jackpot.

D) Holders of the winning tickets that live in different regions of the state will share the jackpot.

14) Which sentence is correct, clear, and concise?

A) Returning from the grocery store on an otherwise uneventful evening, Joan discovered her front door ajar.

B) On an otherwise uneventful evening, Joan discovered her front door ajar, returning from the grocery store.

C) Joan, on an otherwise uneventful evening, returning from the grocery store, discovered her front door ajar.

D) Joan discovered her front door ajar, returning from the grocery store on an otherwise uneventful evening.

15) Which sentence is correct, clear, and concise?
- A) I have always believed that it is important to work hard and be playing hard.
- B) I have always believed in the importance of hard work as well as playing hard.
- C) I have always believed in the importance of working hard and playing hard.

16) Which sentence expresses the thought most clearly and effectively and has no errors in its structure?
- A) Today's military pilots receive environmental education on why noise-sensitive areas should be avoided and the process by which approved airspace is acquired.
- B) Today's military pilots receive environmental education not only on why noise-sensitive areas should be avoided but also the ways approved airspace is acquired.
- C) Today's military pilots receive environmental education on the necessity of avoiding noise-sensitive areas and on the process of acquiring approved airspace.

17) Which sentences expresses the thought most clearly and effectively and has no errors in its structure?
- A) I always hoped I would go to college, but I never dreamed I would graduate with honors.
- B) I always hoped I would go to college, but graduating with honors I only dreamed of.
- C) My hope always was to go to college, but I never dreamed I would graduate with honors.

Choose the correct option to replace the underlined words.

18) Maria Da Silva had read extensively about the United States and spoke fluent English, yet this was the first time she had traveled outside her native Brazil.
- A) English, yet;   B) English yet,   C) English; yet   D) no change

19) Heinrich is a vocal soccer fan; however, most of the time, he is soft-spoken.
- A) fan, however   B) fan, however;   C) fan however,   D) no change

20) Pushing his glasses back to the bridge of his nose. Brent MacDouglas spoke about the joys of calculus.
- A) nose; Brent   B) nose, Brent   C) nose: Brent   D) no change

21) Selwyn tutors his fellow students. Who speak English as a second language.
- A) students who   B) students, who   C) students; who   D) no change

22) Running <u>hard. The</u> thief left the scene of the crime and eluded the police.

    A) hard, the   B) hard; the   C) hard the   D) no change

Choose the correct option to replace the underlined words.

23) Everyone who <u>does</u> not take active precautions for the next hurricane to hit our shores <u>are</u> misguided.

    A) does, is   B) do, is   C) do, are   D) no change

24) One of the executives <u>are</u> attending the sexual harassment seminar while her staff <u>has</u> the day off.

    A) is, have   B) is, has   C) are, have   D) no change

25) Neither the dog nor the cats <u>is</u> going on the trip because Mario and Wanda feel there <u>is</u> not enough room in the car.

    A) are, are   B) are, is   C) is, are   D) no change

26) Each of the students <u>has</u> to give a five-minute speech; in addition, he or she <u>have</u> to use a visual aid.

    A) has, has   B) have, have   C) have, has   D) no change

27) Neither the basketball coach nor <u>him</u> knew why the team could not get <u>itself</u> on track during the first half.

    A) he, itself   B) he, themselves   C) him, themselves   D) no change

28) According to Drabowski, <u>us</u> members have to pick <u>who</u> is going to represent our organization at the convention.

    A) us, whom   B) we, whom   C) we, who   D) no change

29) Juan and <u>I</u> played doubles with Sylvia and <u>he</u>.

    A) I, him   B) me, him   C) me, he   D) no change

30) The football league wants to require all of <u>their</u> players to take random drug tests. If players fail, <u>they</u> will not be allowed to play.

    A) its, they   B) their, he   C) its, he   D) no change

Choose the correct option.

31)

    A. On the radio, it was reported that flooding was most severe in South Carolina and Georgia.

    B. On the radio, they reported that flooding was most severe in South Carolina and Georgia.

    C. On the radio, the most severe flooding was most severe in South Carolina and Georgia.

    D. The radio reported that flooding was most severe in South Carolina and Georgia.

Choose the correct option to replace the underlined words.

32) From the remaining fur, flesh, and bone, we <u>inferred</u> that the raccoon had pried

                                                 A

itself <u>lose</u> from the snare the <u>preceding</u> day.

    B   C

    A) implied   B) loose   C) proceeding   D) no change

33) Everything seemed <u>alright</u> since we had <u>already</u> paid the <u>fare</u>, when we realized

                         A   B   C

that we were on the wrong train.

    A) all right   B) all ready   C) fair   D) no change

34) Because of the large <u>number</u> of trees that were felled, there are now <u>less</u> nesting

                             A   B

<u>sites</u> for the falcons.

C

    A) amount   B) fewer   C) cites   D) no change

Choose the correct option to replace the underlined words.

35) Mr. Patel <u>drank</u> the mango tea that he had <u>set</u> on the table.

    A) drunk, sat B) drinked, set   C) no change

36) If I <u>was</u> free this Friday evening, I <u>would be</u> happy to go to the dance with you.

    A) were, would be   B) were, would have been   C) no change

37) The archeologist <u>would have left</u> next month for Guatemala to explore Mayan ruins <u>had she not broken</u> her leg last week.
          A) will have left, had she not broke
          B) would leave, if she had not broke
          C) no change

38) Which sentence is the most logical and correctly expresses the comparison?
          A) Yvette's grades in math are good as Michelle's.
          B) Yvette's grades in math are as good as Michelle.
          C) Yvette's grades in math are as good as Michelle's.

39) Which sentence is the most logical and correctly expresses the comparison?
          A) The plays of Edward Albee are more controversial than those of Neil Simon.
          B) Edward Albee wrote plays that are more controversial than Neil Simon.
          C) The plays of Edward Albee are more controversial than Neil Simon.

40) Which sentence is the most logical and correctly expresses the comparison?
          A) Phyllis is not smarter than her; Phyllis is just a better student.
          B) Phyllis is not more smarter than her; Phyllis is just a better student.
          C) Phyllis is not smarter than she; Phyllis is just a better student.

Choose the correct option to replace the underlined words.

41) Bill spoke <u>well</u>, even though he did not feel <u>good</u>, and then he walked <u>unsteadily</u>
          A   B   C
off the podium.
          A) good   B) well   C) unsteady   D) no change

42) Jason said he was not <u>real prejudice</u>, but his comments about minorities suggested otherwise.
          A) real prejudiced   B) really prejudiced C) really prejudice   D) no change

Choose the correct option from the answers given.

43) According to <u>Rabbi</u> Jerome M. Epstein, "The wonder of the <u>Old Testament</u> is that it
          A   B
is not only a traditional rock of the <u>jewish</u> faith but a viable book for everyone
                                    C
today."
          A) rabbi   B) old testament   C) Jewish   D) no change

44) The wind was blowing gently from the <u>southwest</u> at noon that <u>Memorial Day</u>; by
                                          A   B
three in the afternoon, tornadoes had devastated the <u>midwest.</u>
                                                      C

    A) Southwest B) memorial day   C) Midwest D) no change

45) Baseball still holds out <u>interest</u> as the national <u>pastime</u> played by <u>atheletes</u> of all
                             A   B   C
ages and abilities.

    A) intrest   B) passtime   C) athletes   D) no change

46) Much to our <u>embarassment</u>, we discovered that we were not <u>eligible</u> for the prize
                A   B
in the <u>mathematics</u> contest.
       C

    A) embarrassment   B) eligable C) mathmatics   D) no change

47) Which sentence is correctly punctuated?
    A) This summer, I plan to visit the following cities in Europe: Bruges, Belgium,
        Rothenberg, Germany, Athens, Greece, and Pompeii, Italy.
    B) This summer, I plan to visit the following cities in Europe: Bruges, Belgium;
        Rothenberg, Germany; Athens, Greece; and Pompeii, Italy.
    C) This summer, I plan to visit the following cities in Europe Bruges, Belgium;
        Rothenberg, Germany; Athens, Greece; and Pompeii, Italy.

48) Which sentence is correctly punctuated?
    A) Although she loved working at the Dolphin Research center; her job was not
        her life.
    B) Although she loved working at the Dolphin Research Center, her job was not
        her life.
    C) She loved working at the Dolphin Research Center, although her job was not
        her life.

Choose the correct option to replace the underlined words.

49) "If you don't <u>mind," Amy said</u> to the waitress, "I would like some milk instead of
cream for my coffee."
    A) "If you don't mind" Amy said   B) "If you don't mind, Amy said
    C) "If you don't mind", Amy said   D) no change

50) We were supposed to depart at <u>noon, however, take-off</u> was delayed by a thunderstorm.

A) noon, however; take-off B) noon; however, take-off
C) noon. However take-off D) no change

Exercises

EXERCISE A: Sentence Grammar and Structure

Select the letter of the answer that best describes the underlined portion of each sentence.

1) In what has been called an earth-shattering discovery, evidence of life on Mars was <u>recently</u> uncovered.
   A) adjective B) adverb   C) noun

2) The announcement of the <u>amazing</u> discovery came at a NASA news conference.
   A) adjective B) adverb   C) noun

3) The evidence comes from a 4.2-pound meteorite <u>that</u> was found in Antarctica in 1984.
   A) noun   B) relative pronoun   C) conjunctive adverb

4) Within the <u>interior</u> fissures of the meteorite, scientists found sections of carbonate.
   A) possessive noun B) adverb   C) adjective

5) These <u>sections</u> contained tubular structures similar to microscopic fossils of bacteria.
   A) predicate B) adjective C) subject

6) Scientists found concentrated hydrocarbons, iron sulfides, and magnetite <u>around the possible fossils</u>.
   A) independent clause   B) prepositional phrase   C) participle phrase

7) Hydrocarbons are often found in sediment around decaying organisms, and <u>iron sulfides and magnetite are compounds produced by microorganisms</u>.
   A) independent clause   B) dependent clause   C) relative clause

8) David S. McKay, <u>a planetary scientist</u>, led the team that made the discovery.
   A) dependent clause   B) independent clause   C) appositive

9) He says the combination of data is compelling enough to claim the team has discovered <u>evidence</u> of past life.
   A) subject   B) predicate C) object

10) <u>While the team of scientists has not found "the smoking gun,"</u> it believes its Martian life theory offers the simplest explanation.
    A) dependent clause   B) independent clause   C) participle phrase

91

11) Many in the scientific community are excited by the team's discovery; <u>however</u>, not all of them agree that the evidence is conclusive.

      A) subordinating conjunction   B) coordinating conjunction

      C) conjunctive adverb

12) Some scientists are skeptical <u>because</u> the compounds found on the meteorite have also been found on meteorites that weren't from Mars.

      A) subordinating conjunction   B) coordinating conjunction

      C) conjunctive adverb

13) In spite of the controversy, the discovery will most likely speed up NASA's plans <u>to send</u> probes to Mars.

      A) prepositional phrase   B) infinitive verb   C) adverb

14) <u>Hoping to capitalize on the team's discovery,</u> NASA plans to send several unmanned expeditions to Mars in the next ten to fifteen years.

      A) independent clause   B) dependent clause   C) participle phrase

15) These will be followed by a manned expedition to <u>Mars</u> in the second decade of the twenty-first century.

      A) proper noun   B) collective noun   C) subject

EXERCISE B: Using Verbs

Select the letter of the correct verb.

1) In the early 1970s, the United States _____ to experience a new wave of immigration.

    A) began   B) begun   C) begins

2) Since the 1970s, approximately 800,000 legal and 300,000 illegal new immigrants _____ the United States.

    A) are entering   B) have entered   C) enter

3) As a result, between 1970 and 1998 the percentage of immigrants in the United States _____ from 4.8% to 8.9%.

    A) rose   B) raised   C) was rising

4) Until recently, most of the new immigrants _____ from Asia, Latin America, and the Caribbean.

    A) come   B) came   C) are coming

5) Large numbers of the new immigrants have _____ to live in New York, Texas, Florida, or California.

    A) chose   B) chosed   C) chosen

6) By the late 1990s, after years of unrestricted traffic, the large number of immigrants _____ a financial burden for these states.

    A) became   B) had become   C) has become

7) Until then, welfare agencies, health care facilities, and school systems _____ the brunt of the pressure.

    A) had borne   B) bore   C) have borne

8) People say these agencies are hard-pressed to provide services now that tax dollars _____.

    A) dry up   B) had dried up   C) are drying up

9) Some people want to place limits on immigration because they fear that today illegal immigrants _____ jobs away from citizens.

    A) are taking   B) would take   C) have been taking

10) Some _____ about how new immigrants might assimilate in a nation whose people are mainly European.

      A) are concerned   B) are concern   C) have been concern

11) Soon after complaints arose, Congress _____ various proposals to limit the number of immigrants admitted each year.

      A) could consider   B) is considering   C) considered

12) If some of the legislation _____, immigrants would be denied many benefits citizens take for granted.

      A) was passed   B) were passed   C) would be passed

13) Some of the bills proposed in the late 1990s _____ no distinction between legal and illegal immigrants.

      A) made   B) have been making   C) were making

14) If some of these laws are applied rigidly, legal immigrants _____ to take their children out of public school.

      A) were forced   B) will be forced   C) are being forced

15) Some school districts in California said that they _____ to comply, if laws were applied to deny an education to illegal immigrants.

      A) would refuse   B) refuse   C) will refuse

EXERCISE C: Case of Pronouns and Nouns

Select the letter of the choice that represents the correct use of the pronoun case.

1) John, Cathy, and _____ like to go to rock concerts.
   A) I   B) me

2) John prefers the "classic" groups like the Eagles and the Who, both of _____ have had reunion tours.
   A) who   B) whom

3) Between you and _____, I think these groups are passé.
   A) I   B) me

4) I prefer somewhat more contemporary groups such as the Cranberries and Hootie and the Blowfish, but I have to admit, _____ sounds are similar to some old groups that John likes.
   A) they're   B) their   C) there

5) One group that never seemed to go out of vogue, although _____ music never changed from the sixties, was the Grateful Dead.
   A) its   B) their   C) there

6) For a long time, John and Cathy were Deadheads, people _____ travel from city to city following the Grateful Dead on tour.
   A) that   B) whom   C) who

7) To John and _____, the Grateful Dead embodied all the vices and virtues of the sixties.
   A) she   B) her

8) Free love, communal living, pacifism, mind-expansion through drugs, _____ the values the Dead professed.
   A) these are   B) this is

9) _____ three did not always agree about the values the Dead stood for, but we sure loved the band's music.
   A) Us   B) We

95

10) We also loved the atmosphere surrounding the Dead's concerts as much as the concerts _____.

    A) themself B) theirself C) themselves

11) The Volkswagen buses plastered with peace and flower-power decals, the people selling Dead paraphernalia, the sharing of food and resources, no one enjoyed these more than _____.

    A) we   B) us   C) ours

12) Cathy's favorite member of the band was Jerry Garcia, _____ lifestyle was the embodiment of excess.

    A) who's B) whom C) whose

13) When he died, I was deeply saddened, but I didn't take it nearly as hard as _____.

    A) she   B) her

14) Some people felt his death marked the end of the Dead, but I think _____ wrong.

    A) their   B) there   C) they're

15) The spirit of the band lives on in its music and in fans like John, Cathy, and _____.

    A) I   B) me

EXERCISE D: Using Adjectives and Adverbs

Select the letter of the correct answer.

1) Some Americans were _____ that the English language is losing ground in the United States.

    A) real worried   B) really worried

2) They believed that legislation was _____ needed to guarantee English as the nation's standard language.

    A) bad   B) badly

3) A bill before the Senate, the English Language Empowerment Act, would make English an _____ sanctioned language.

    A) official   B) officially

4) However, linguists point to the worldwide use of English as _____ in the history of languages.

    A) most unique   B) more unique   C) unique

5) They argue that fears of a decline in the use of English should not be taken _____.

    A) too serious   B) to seriously   C) too seriously

6) About one-fifth of the world's population now speaks English _____ enough to communicate.

    A) good   B) well

7) The number of people who speak English as a second language is growing _____.

    A) really quick   B) real quickly   C) really quickly

8) The use of English is _____ throughout much of Asia and Africa.

    A) widespread   B) wide spread out   C) spreaded widely

9) In a number of countries where numerous languages and dialects are spoken, English has some _____ advantages for language factions trying to communicate among themselves.

    A) terribly practical B) very practical

10) Technology has also had a _____ impact on the spread of English throughout the world.

      A) dramatic   B) dramatical   C) dramatized

11) The Internet provides _____ opportunities that could not have been imagined a few years ago.

      A) education B) educational

12) However, students must have a _____ grasp of English to avail themselves of these opportunities.

      A) reasonably good   B) reasonable good   C) real good

13) Because the Internet's linguistic patterns and best software are in English, it is _____ to carry on an electronic relationship without knowledge of English.

      A) near impossible   B) nearly impossible

14) However, this situation most likely won't last long because changes in the Internet occur _____ for English to remain its only international language.

      A) too quickly   B) to quickly   C) too quick

15) Because English has become the international language of commerce, communication, and scientific discourse, people who are _____ about its status have nothing to worry about.

      A) real concerned   B) real concern   C) really concerned

EXERCISE E: Revising for Subject-Verb Agreement

Select the letter of the correct verb.

1) Everyone, at one time or another, _____ seen pictures of tornadoes.
   A) has   B) have

2) These storms, intense whirlwinds shaped like a funnel, _____ among the most destructive forces in nature.
   A) is   B) are

3) They usually form between April and June when masses of cool, dry air from Canada _____ with warm, moist air from the Gulf of Mexico.
   A) collide   B) collides

4) Carrying winds in excess of 200 miles per hour, one of these storms _____ capable of leveling whole towns.
   A) is   B) are

5) Each year there _____ about 1,000 tornadoes reported in the United States.
   A) is   B) are

6) In one year alone, property damage caused by tornadoes _____ estimated at close to half a billion dollars.
   A) was   B) were

7) Since 1900, a large number of Americans, 10,000 to be exact, _____ died in tornadoes.
   A) has   B) have

8) Although many people believe that a tornado, also known as a twister, _____ only in the Midwest, one can occur in almost every part of the country.
   A) develop   B) develops

9) When a twister or a tornado _____ over water, it is called a water spout.
   A) form   B) forms

10) Scientists known as storm chasers _____ been closely following tornadoes to learn how they are formed.

    A) has   B) have

11) The film *Twister* follows a team of scientists that _____ after these dangerous storms.

    A) chase   B) chases

12) Unlike the scientists who _____ these storms in real life, the film's storm chasers get within a few hundred yards of the tornadoes.

    A) follow   B) follows

13) Anyone who has experienced these intense storms _____ better than to get so close.

    A) know   B) knows

14) They don't want to end up like the cow in *Twister* or any of the other objects that _____ caught up in the storm and hurled through space.

    A) is   B) are

EXERCISE F: Revising for Sentence Fragments

Choose the sentence that does not contain a sentence fragment and is punctuated correctly.

1)

    A) Most authorities on the subject trace the origins of the detective story to Edgar Allan Poe. The nineteenth century short story writer, critic, and poet who wrote "The Raven."

    B) Most authorities on the subject trace the origins of the detective story to Edgar Allan Poe, the nineteenth-century short story writer, critic, and poet who wrote "The Raven."

    C) Most authorities on the subject trace the origins of the detective story to Edgar Allan Poe, the nineteenth century short story writer, critic, and poet. Who wrote "The Raven."

2)

    A) In the 1840s Poe wrote stories that established many of the conventions of the genre. Such as "The Murders in the Rue Morgue," "The Mystery of Marie Roget," and "The Purloined Letter."

    B) In the 1840s Poe wrote stories that established many of the conventions of the genre. For example, "The Murders in the Rue Morgue," "The Mystery of Marie Roget," and "The Purloined Letter."

    C) In the 1840s Poe wrote stories that established many of the conventions of the genre, such as "The Murders in the Rue Morgue," "The Mystery of Marie Roget," and "The Purloined Letter."

3)

    A) In "The Murders in the Rue Morgue," Poe created C. Auguste Dupin, fiction's first amateur detective.

    B) In "The Murders in the Rue Morgue," Poe created C. Auguste Dupin fiction's first amateur detective.

    C) In "The Murders in the Rue Morgue," Poe created C. Auguste Dupin. Who was fiction's first amateur detective.

4)

    A) Poe also created the convention of the narrator who is an admiring friend. A device that was later made famous by Sir Arthur Conan Doyle.

    B) Poe also created the convention of the narrator who is an admiring friend. This device was later made famous by Sir Arthur Conan Doyle.

    C) Poe also created the convention of the narrator. An admiring friend and a device that was later made famous by Sir Arthur Conan Doyle.

5)

A) In honor of Sherlock Holmes' friend and chronicler. These narrators are now referred to as Watsons.

B) In honor of Sherlock Holmes' friend and chronicler; these narrators are now referred to as Watsons.

C) In honor of Sherlock Holmes' friend and chronicler, these narrators are now referred to as Watsons.

6)

A) Poe also established the following conventions. The locked room mystery, the accusations of an innocent suspect, and the trap set for the real perpetrator.

B) Poe also established the following conventions, the locked room mystery, the accusations of an innocent suspect, and the trap set for the real perpetrator.

C) Poe also established the following conventions: the locked room mystery, the accusations of an innocent suspect, and the trap set for the real perpetrator.

7)

A) Poe also invented the convention of the solution that is overlooked. Because it is so obvious.

B) Poe also invented the convention of the solution that is overlooked because it is so obvious.

C) Poe also invented the convention of the solution that is overlooked, because it is so obvious.

8)

A) The pitting of detective against bumbling police officer was yet another convention Poe invented.

B) The pitting of detective against bumbling police officer. It was yet another convention Poe invented.

C) The pitting of detective against bumbling police officer was yet another convention. Which Poe invented.

9)

A) There are several sub-genres of detective fiction. For instance, private eye mysteries, police procedurals, hard-boiled mysteries, locked room mysteries, and thrillers.

B) There are several sub-genres of detective fiction, such as private eye mysteries, police procedurals, hard-boiled mysteries, locked room mysteries, and thrillers.

C) There are several sub-genres of detective fiction. Including private eye mysteries, police procedurals, hard-boiled mysteries, locked room mysteries, and thrillers.

10)

    A) The locked room mystery was perfected by John Dickenson Carr. Generally regarded as the greatest plot magician.

    B) The locked room mystery was perfected by John Dickenson Carr, he is generally regarded as the greatest plot magician.

    C) The locked room mystery was perfected by John Dickenson Carr, who is generally regarded as the greatest plot magician.

11)

    A) In a locked room mystery, where not only is the crime committed in a room with locked windows and doors. But the room is also watched by witnesses.

    B) In a locked room mystery, not only is the crime committed in a room with locked windows and doors. But also watched by witnesses.

    C) In a locked room mystery, not only is the crime committed in a room with locked windows and doors, but the room is also watched by witnesses.

12)

    A) Inventing dozens of ways of entering and exiting the locked room, Carr never once used a secret passage!

    B) Inventing dozens of ways of entering and exiting the locked room. Carr never once used a secret passage!

    C) Though he invented dozens of ways of entering and exiting a locked room. Carr never once used a secret passage!

EXERCISE G: Comma Splices and Fused Sentences

Choose the letter of the selection that creates neither a comma splice nor a fused sentence.

1) The U.S. Patent Office opened in 1838 it has granted more patents for mouse traps than for any other invention.

    A) 1838, it   B) 1838; it   C) no change

2) The Patent Office grants about forty new mouse trap patents a year it turns down ten times as many applications.

    A) year; but   B) year but   C) year, but

3) Thousands of mouse traps have been patented, only a few have made money for their inventors.

    A) patented; however,   B) patented, however;   C) no change

4) Some early traps impaled, choked, or drowned mice, more recent inventions have electrocuted or gassed them.

    A) mice; whereas, more   B) mice; more   C) no change

5) Successful choker traps lured a mouse into sticking its head through a hole then used a wire noose to choke it.

    A) hole, then used   B) hole. Then used   C) hole; then they used

6) Not every mouse trap is designed to kill mice, some only trap them.

    A) mice; some   B) mice, and   C) no change

7) In the 1870s, a number of "toy traps" were patented these lured the mouse into some sort of spinning, turning, or rolling mechanism.

    A) patented, these   B) patented; these   C) no change

8) The mechanisms were similar to the plastic bubbles and exercise wheels found in today's small mammal habitats but once a mouse entered the toy trap, it could not escape.

    A) habitats, but   B) habitats but,   C) no change

9) The most successful mouse trap was patented in 1903 by John Mast, it is still manufactured today.

    A) Mast, which   B) Mast. It   C) no change

105

10) Mast's trap uses a striking method a spring-activated metal rod breaks the mouse's neck.

    A) method, a   B) method: a   C) no change

11) Mast manufactured coleslaw and popcorn, one can see why he needed a mouse trap with foods that mice liked to eat on the premises.

    A) popcorn, so   B) popcorn; so   C) no change

12) Mast's trap has maintained its popularity for three reasons, it was simple, cheap to produce, and killed instantly.

    A) reasons it   B) reasons: it   C) no change

13) Electric mouse traps had one fatal flaw in their design, they were potentially dangerous to children and pets.

    A) design. They   B) design, which they   C) no change

14) The cheap cost of the snap trap is important because Americans do not remove the mouse and reset the trap, they drop the trap and the mouse into the trash.

    A) trap: they   B) trap; they   C) no change

15) This practice is entirely unnecessary; but, it makes the manufacturers very happy.

    A) unnecessary but it   B) unnecessary but, it   C) unnecessary, but it

EXERCISE H: Revising Misplaced and Dangling Modifiers

In each of the following sets, choose the letter of the sentence that expresses the thought most clearly and effectively.

1)
   A) People have inhabited a small cavern in Australia's Kakadu National Park for over 20,000 years continuously.
   B) People have continuously inhabited a small cavern in Australia's Kakadu National Park for over 20,000 years.

2)
   A) Aborigines called the Gagudju lived there only a mere dozen years ago.
   B) Aborigines called the Gagudju only lived there a mere dozen years ago.

3)
   A) Looking at the floor and in every corner of the cavern carefully, I saw stone tools and the bones of animals.
   B) Looking carefully at the floor and in every corner of the cavern, I saw stone tools and the bones of animals.

4)
   A) Lying near these artifacts are more recently used objects, such as beer cans, styrofoam cups, and plastic wrappers.
   B) Lying near these artifacts are objects, such as beer cans, styrofoam cups, and plastic wrappers.

5)
   A) The Gagudju now have abandoned the cavern and live in another part of the park.
   B) The Gagudju have abandoned the cavern and now live in another part of the park.

6)
   A) The first time I visited the cavern, I only saw a painting of a fish on the wall.
   B) The first time I visited the cavern, I saw only a painting of a fish on the wall.

7)
   A) However, beside the fish there are paintings of spiny anteaters, goats, and pigs drawn finely.
   B) However, beside the fish there are finely drawn paintings of spiny anteaters, goats, and pigs.

8)

    A) Driving all day through the park, I came to the camp of the Gagudju who once lived at the site of the cavern.

    B) I came to the camp of the Gagudju after driving all day through the park who once lived near the site of the cavern.

9)

    A) Sitting cross-legged under a shady tree, there are several Aborigines who greet me.

    B) Sitting cross-legged under a shady tree, several Aborigines greet me.

10)

    A) Listening to their stories, they are the only ones I realize who can tell me about the Gagudju culture.

    B) Listening to their stories, I realize that they are the only ones who can tell me about the Gagudju's culture.

11)

    A) Never having been written down, these few old men possess the ancient knowledge of their people.

    B) Never having been written down, the ancient knowledge of their people is possessed by these few old men.

12)

    A) The elders speak in short sentences softly.

    B) The elders speak softly in short sentences.

13)

    A) They tell me about the time of the creation, called the Dreamtime, when ancestral beings created the land and gave birth to the people.

    B) Called the Dreamtime, they tell me about the time of the creation when ancestral beings created the land and gave birth to the people.

14)

    A) When the ancestral beings completed the creation, they told the Gagudju to not change anything.

    B) When the ancestral beings completed the creation, they told the Gagudju not to change anything.

15)

    A) They told the Gagudju to live in harmony with the land.

    B) They told the Gagudju to live with the land in harmony.

EXERCISE I: Revising for Shifts and Mixed Construction

The following sentences describe a process that hunter "Jack Doe" might follow. Select the letter of the answer that is consistent in person, number, tense, voice (active or passive), and mood (statement or command).

1) Let us assume that a man named Jack Doe has just successfully killed a buck. After that hunter kills a deer or any other large game, _____ a process called Field Care to save the animal's meat.

    A) they must use   B) he must use   C) you must use

2) In the first step, the hunter positions the deer with its head and shoulders below its rump, and then _____ a cut from the hind legs to the pelvic bone.

    A) he made   B) they make   C) he makes

3) With the first step complete, _____ a cut up the middle of the stomach all the way to the breast bone.

    A) the hunter makes B) the hunter made   C) the hunter can make

4) When the hunter completes this cut, _____ through the muscle wall.

    A) you slice   B) slice   C) he slices

5) Using a sharp knife or hand saw, the hunter cuts the cartilage connecting the sides of the breast bone, and then _____ the pelvic bone.

    A) he splits   B) they will split   C) split

6) In the next step, the hunter _____ the windpipe as close to the head as possible.

    A) has cut   B) cuts   C) would cut

7) Grasping the windpipe in both hands, _____ hard toward the hind quarters.

    A) pull   B) the hunter pulls   C) the hunters pull

8) When the hunter completes this step, _____ through the pelvic opening.

    A) the large intestine is pulled
    B) the large intestine was pulled
    C) he pulls the large intestine

9) If a tree _____, the hunter then hangs the deer by its head or antlers from a branch so the blood drains out.

        A) was handy   B) is handy   C) were to be handy

10) If _____, he turns the animal with its underside down and waits 20 minutes while the blood drains out.

        A) a suitable tree cannot be found
        B) the hunter couldn't find a suitable tree
        C) the hunter cannot find a suitable tree

11) Next, _____ the deer.

        A) the hunters skin   B) the hunter skinned   C) the hunter skins

12) To do this, _____ a cut the full length of each leg and all the way around the neck.

        A) the hunter would make   B) the hunter makes C) the hunter made

13) With both hands grasping the skin at the back of the neck, _____.

        A) the hunter pulls hard   B) you pull hard   C) the hunters pull hard

14) In the final step, cooling, _____.

        A) the carcass is wrapped
        B) the hunter wraps the carcass
        C) wrap the carcass

15) Unless a hunter _____ this process, he could not expect to save as much as 95% of the useable meat.

        A) might follow   B) were to follow   C) was following

EXERCISE J: Revising for Pronoun *References* and Antecedent Agreement

Select the answer that corrects the error in pronoun reference or antecedent agreement.

1) When a chimpanzee first sees their reflection in a mirror, the chimp will behave as if it were encountering another chimp.

      A) its reflection   B) they were   C) no change

2) Soon the chimp will perform simple, repetitive movements while observing their mirrored images closely.

      A) they're   B) its   C) it's

3) The chimps may realize the connection between their behaviors and that of the stranger in the mirror.

      A) its behavior   B) those of   C) no change

4) In the next stage, the chimp turns its attention to themself.

      A) their attention   B) themselves   C) itself

5) The chimp examines itself in the mirror, looking at parts it can't normally see, such as their lips and gums.

      A) themself   B) they can't   C) its lips

6) This suggests that chimpanzees have a high level of self-awareness.

      A) This behavior suggests   B) It suggests   C) no change

7) When mirrors are placed in the cage of a pair of macaques, each of the monkeys will continue to act as if it were confronting another macaque.

      A) they were   B) their confronting   C) no change

8) This is called "empathy."

      A) It is   B) This awareness   C) no change

9) These include hiding food from companions and concealing "illicit" sexual encounters.

      A) They include   B) These behaviors   C) no change

10) While a chimpanzee is an expert at manipulating behavior of others, they seem to have no concept of what others may be thinking.
    A) it seems to have no
    B) they seem not to have any
    C) no change

11) Which sentence is correct, clear, and concise?
    A) It appears that they do not have the same level of self-awareness as chimps and other higher primates.
    B) Apparently, macaques do not have the same level of self-awareness as chimps and other higher primates.

12) Which sentence is correct, clear, and concise?
    A) To determine their level of self-awareness, researchers examine other aspects of ape behavior.
    B) To determine the level of self-awareness in apes, researchers examine other aspects of their behavior.
    C) Researchers examine other aspects of primate behavior to determine the level of self-awareness in apes.

13) Which sentence is correct, clear, and concise?
    A) In one study of primate social interaction, it was reported that they engage in apparent deceptions.
    B) One study of primate social interaction reported that chimpanzees engage in apparent deceptions.
    C) In one study of primate social interaction, researchers reported that they engage in apparent deceptions.

14) Which sentence is correct, clear, and concise?
    A) Researchers have also performed experiments with primates to determine whether or not they are aware of the mental states of others.
    B) To determine whether or not they are aware of the mental states of others, researchers have also performed experiments with primates.
    C) Researchers have performed experiments with primates to determine whether or not apes are aware of the mental states of others.

15) Which sentence is correct, clear, and concise?
    A) In a human, empathy develops when they are in the toddler stage.
    B) In humans, empathy develops in the toddler stage.
    C) Empathy it is developed in humans in the toddler stage.

EXERCISE K: Mixed or Incomplete Sentences

In each of the following pairs of sentences, choose the sentence that is correct and effective.

1)
    A) The historical Dracula, a prince called Vlad, he ruled the Romanian region of Wallachia in the fifteenth century.
    B) The historical Dracula, a prince called Vlad, ruled the Romanian region of Wallachia in the fifteenth century.

2)
    A) Because he impaled his enemies, he became known as Vlad the Impaler
    B) Because he impaled his enemies became known as Vlad the Impaler.

3)
    A) The nickname Dracula, meaning dragon, it was given to him because of his brutal rule.
    B) The nickname Dracula, meaning dragon, was given to him because of his brutal rule.

4)
    A) The fact that he defeated the Turks some Romanians regard him as a hero.
    B) Because he defeated the Turks, some Romanians regard him as a hero.

5)
    A) In most early stories about him, his heroic deeds were emphasized.
    B) In most early stories about him emphasized his heroic deeds.

6)
    A) In the novel *Dracula* by Bram Stoker is when his modern image emerged.
    B) In the novel *Dracula* by Bram Stoker, his modern image emerged.

7)
    A) The novel depicts Dracula as a corpse who turns into a blood-sucking bat at night.
    B) The novel depicts Dracula as a corpse and turns into a blood-sucking bat at night.

8)

A) Shortly after the publication of the novel was followed by a London stage version.

B) Shortly after the publication of the novel, a London stage version followed.

9)

A) In the German silent film *Nosferatu* (1923) was when Dracula made him a star.

B) In the German silent film *Nosferatu* (1923), Dracula first appeared on screen.

10)

A) Bela Lugosi's memorable performance in the 1931 film *Dracula* made him a star.

B) Because of Bela Lugosi's memorable performance in the 1931 film *Dracula* made him a star.

11)

A) The fact that Lugosi's Transylvanian accent added to the film's authenticity.

B) The fact that Lugosi had a Transylvanian accent added to the film's authenticity.

12)

A) Bela Lugosi was one actor who became famous playing Dracula; Gary Oldman was another.

B) Bela Lugosi was one actor who became famous playing Dracula, Gary Oldman another.

13)

A) No other monster has left such a strong impression on the public, perhaps Frankenstein.

B) No other monster, with the possible exception of Frankenstein, has left such a strong impression on the public.

14)

A) None of the fictional Draculas has committed deeds horrible as those committed by Vlad the Impaler.

B) None of the fictional Draculas has committed deeds as horrible as those committed by Vlad the Impaler.

15)

A) Sometimes, real "monsters" are more frightening.

B) Sometimes, real "monsters" are more frightening than fictional ones.

EXERCISE L: Revising for Coordination, Subordination, and Emphasis

In each of the following sets, choose the letter of the most effective sentence.

1)
    A) The Federal Aviation Administration has two functions, and these are to promote and regulate the airline industry.
    B) The Federal Aviation Administration has two functions, which are the promotion and regulation of the airline industry.
    C) The two functions of the Federal Aviation Administration are to promote and regulate the airline industry.

2)
    A) The FAA has many critics, and they argue that these functions are not compatible.
    B) There are many critics of the FAA; however, they argue that these functions are not compatible.
    C) The FAA has many critics who argue that these functions are not compatible.

3)
    A) Critics also complain that many FAA administrators maintain close ties with the airline industry which they used to work for.
    B) Critics also complain that many FAA administrators who used to work for the airline industry, and they maintain close ties with it.
    C) Critics complain that many FAA administrators who used to work for the airline industry maintain close ties with it.

4)
    A) Moreover, critics charge that the FAA drags its feet instead of forcing airlines to adopt new technology.
    B) Another charge that critics level at the FAA is that the agency drags its feet instead of forcing airlines to adopt new technology.
    C) There is another charge leveled by critics, and that is the agency drags its feet instead of forcing airlines to adopt new technology.

5)

    A) Another reason why the FAA has been criticized is because it has been slow to monitor the airline industry's growing reliance on outside contractors.

    B) The airline industry has grown increasingly reliant on outside contractors, and the FAA has also been criticized because it has been slow to monitor this development.

    C) The FAA has also been criticized because it has been slow to monitor the airline industry's growing reliance on outside contractors.

6)

    A) This common practice is called "outsourcing," which can cut costs, but can also lead to cut-rate care.

    B) This is a common practice called "outsourcing," and even though it can cut costs, it can also lead to cut-rate care.

    C) Although this common practice, called "outsourcing," can cut costs, it can also lead to cut-rate care.

7)

    A) The practice of outsourcing services such as maintenance and reservations has created "virtual airlines."

    B) Airlines have outsourced services such as maintenance and reservations, and by doing so, they have created "virtual airlines."

    C) Airlines have outsourced services such as maintenance and reservations, which have created "virtual airlines."

8)

    A) Another criticism leveled against the FAA is that it has not acted quickly enough to counter the threat of attacks against U.S. airlines.

    B) Another criticism has been leveled against the FAA, and that is it has not acted quickly enough to counter the threat of attack against U.S. airlines.

    C) Another criticism has been leveled against the FAA, which is the agency has not acted quickly enough to counter the threat of attack against U.S. airlines.

9)

    A) In 1993 and 1995, the U.S. Department of Transportation sent teams to penetrate areas of major U.S. airports that were supposed to be secure; however, the teams were successful in three out of four attempts.

    B) In 1993 and 1995, the U.S. Department of Transportation sent teams to penetrate areas of major U.S. airports that were supposed to be secure, and the teams were successful in three out of four attempts.

    C) In 1993 and 1995 the U.S. Department of Transportation sent teams to penetrate areas of major U.S. airports that were suppose to be secure, which were successful in three out of four attempts.

10)

    A) Also, in 1990 Congress set a goal for the FAA to develop new technologies for detecting high-tech bombs, which the agency failed to meet.

    B) Also, in 1990 Congress set a goal for the FAA to develop new technologies for detecting high-tech bombs, but the agency failed to meet the goal.

    C) Also, in 1990 Congress set a goal for the FAA, and the goal was to develop new technologies for detecting high-tech bombs, but the agency failed to meet the goal.

EXERCISE M: Writing and Revising to Achieve Parallelism

In each of the following sets, choose the sentence with the best parallel structure.

1)
   A) She was stocky, she was built for the cold and enormously strong.
   B) She was stocky, built for the cold, and enormously strong.
   C) She was stocky, built for the cold, and she was enormously strong.

2)
   A) She had a broad nose, thick brow ridges, and a low forehead.
   B) She had a broad nose, her brow ridges were thick, and a low forehead.
   C) She had a broad nose, brow ridges that were thick, and her forehead was low.

3)
   A) She may have practiced cannibalism, but she also may have been a nurturer of the sick.
   B) She may have been a practicing cannibal, but she may also have nurtured the sick.
   C) She may have practiced cannibalism, but she also may have nurtured the sick.

4)
   A) She was a Neanderthal, a highly resourceful, highly intelligent creature.
   B) She was a Neanderthal, a creature with high intelligence and resourceful.
   C) She was a Neanderthal, a highly resourceful creature, and intelligent.

5)
   A) Neanderthals roamed throughout Europe as far north as Britain and south to Spain.
   B) Neanderthals roamed throughout Europe north as far as Britain and as far south as Spain.
   C) Neanderthals roamed throughout Europe as far north as Britain and as far south as Spain.

6)
   A) Neanderthals were tool users, wore clothing, and also they buried their dead.
   B) Neanderthals used tools, wore clothing and their dead were buried.
   C) Neanderthals used tools, wore clothing, and buried their dead.

7)

    A) They hunted in groups, they gathered edible plants, and were fisherman.

    B) They hunted in groups, gathered edible plants, and caught fish.

    C) They were group hunters, edible plant gatherers, and they fished.

8)

    A) Their bones tell us they had a lot of strength and the ability to endure.

    B) Their bones tell us they had a lot of strength and endurance.

    C) Their bones tell us they were strong and had endurance.

9)

    A) Their remains show evidence of broken bones, neck trauma, and head injuries.

    B) Their remains show evidence of bones that were broken, neck trauma, and they had head injuries.

    C) Their remains show evidence of bones that were broken, necks that had trauma, and head injuries.

10)

    A) Bone fragments tell us what was eaten by Neanderthals and what they looked like.

    B) Bone fragments tell us what Neanderthals looked like and their eating habits.

    C) Bone fragments tell us what Neanderthals looked like and what they ate.

11)

    A) They had tools for cutting, to butcher, and to scrape.

    B) They had tools for cutting, butchering, and scraping.

    C) They had tools for cutting, also butchering, and to scrape.

12)

    A) To make tools and to organize a hunt, Neanderthals and modern man must have been able to communicate.

    B) Making tools and to organize a hunt, Neanderthals and modern man must have been able to communicate.

    C) To make tools and for organizing a hunt, Neanderthals and modern man must have communicated.

13)
   A) Both races lived side by side, their hunting was similar, and they buried their dead in the manner.
   B) Both races lived side by side, and their hunting was similar as were their burial practices.
   C) Both races lived side by side, hunted the same way, and buried their dead in the same manner.

14)
   A) Did early humans kill Neanderthals, intermarry with them, or outbreed them?
   B) Did early humans kill Neanderthals, did they intermarry with them, or were the Neanderthals outbred by them?
   C) Did early modern humans kill the Neanderthals, intermarry with them, or did they have more children?

EXERCISE N: Diction, Choosing the Right Word

Select the letter of the word whose meaning fits the context of the sentence. Selection should be appropriate for the semi-formal tone used in college essays and term papers.

1) In 1924, Nathan Leopold and Richard Loeb _____ a young boy named Robert Franks.

    A) wasted   B) murdered   C) blew away

2) Their _____ crime was the first to be called "the crime of the century."

    A) heinous   B) prodigious   C) awesome

3) Leopold and Loeb came from two of the most _____ families in Chicago.

    A) conspicuous   B) noticeable   C) prominent

4) Both young men were highly _____, having graduated from high school by the age of fifteen.

    A) intelligent   B) brainy   C) sharp

5) Conversant in several languages, Leopold was a _____ linguist.

    A) unobjectionable   B) top-notch   C) gifted

6) They both believed they were _____ beings who were not bound by the rules that govern ordinary people.

    A) outstanding   B) excellent   C) superior

7) Their families hired Clarence Darrow, a(n) _____ defense attorney who was experienced in civil rights cases.

    A) famous   B) notorious   C) infamous

8) During their trial, Leopold and Loeb showed no _____ for their crime.

    A) guilt   B) remorse   C) sorrow

9) By defending them, Darrow hoped to strike a _____ blow against capital punishment.

    A) lethal   B) killer   C) deathly

10) The over-matched district attorney was consistently _____ by Darrow's courtroom tactics.

      A) outmaneuvered   B) aced out   C) blown away

11) The district attorney insisted that Leopold and Loeb were high-stakes gamblers who kidnapped Franks for ransom, a strategy that _____.

      A) rebounded   B) backfired   C) misconnected

12) Darrow's _____ attack on capital punishment captivated the courtroom.

      A) hysterical   B) passionate   C) frenzied

13) The public was completely _____ the crime and the trial.

      A) obsessed with   B) seduced by   C) discontented with

14) Although there were no riots when Leopold and Loeb received life sentences, the public _____ disagreed with the judge's decision.

      A) vehemently   B) brutally   C) feverishly

15) The Leopold and Loeb case bears many striking _____ to the most recent "crime of the century," the O.J. Simpson murder trial.

      A) likenesses   B) resemblances   C) similitudes

EXERCISE O: Learning the Conventions of Spelling

Select the letter of the choice with the correct spelling.

1) Looking at a koala, Australia's favorite marsupial, has a strange affect on the psyches of many people.

    A) marsupeal   B) effect   C) pysches

2) They believe these furry creatures are quiet harmless.

    A) belive   B) cretures   C) quite

3) However, these national ikons have bad tempers and are often grumpy.

    A) icons   B) tempors   C) grummpy

4) In the wild, these pecular pseudo bears could rip a person to pieces.

    A) peculiar   B) seudo   C) peaces

5) Unfortunately, the koala bear is facing extinscion.

    A) Unfortunatly   B) faceing   C) extinction

6) Koalas are susceptible to devestation and disease.

    A) susceptable   B) devastation   C) desease

7) Seperated by housing developments, fields, and shopping centers, their numbers are dwindling.

    A) Separated   B) feilds   C) shoping

8) Eucalyptus leafs are the koala's only food, and eucalyptus forests are rapidly disappearing.

    A) leaves   B) forrests   C) disapearing

9) Aboriginies once hunted koalas to supplement their diets.

    A) Aborigines   B) suppliment   C) there

10) European settlers poisoned hugh numbers of koalas for the animal's valuable pelts.

    A) posioned   B) huge   C) valueable

11) As late as 1927, open hunting seasons yeilded hundreds of thousands of pelts.

    A) yielded   B) hunderds   C) thousinds

12) Opinion polls show that Australians are in dispear over the koala's future.

    A) Opinon   B) poles   C) despair

13) They say what has happened to the koala is a tragedy caused by an insensitive goverment.

    A) tradgedy   B) insensative   C) government

14) However, koalas are now being fitted with radio collars and tracked by recievers.

    A) been   B) fited   C) receivers

15) Veterinarians are drawing blood of captured koalas to test the animal's respons to vaccine.

    A) Vetinarians   B) response   C) vaccine

EXERCISE P: Using End Punctuation

Select the letter of the choice that correctly punctuates the sentence.

1) Asked what word came to mind when he thought of the Internet, one third-world subscriber responded, "Colonialism"

    A) "Colonialism"!   B) "Colonialism!"   C) "Colonialism?"

2) Why would the Internet, a collection of more than 10 million computers that moves data among almost 200 nations, be considered a form of colonialism

    A) colonialism.   B) colonialism!   C) colonialism?

3) The answer, according to some critics of the system, is that the Internet exports the English language (carrying with it immense cultural power)

    A) language.   B) power.)   C) power).

4) Complaining that it is easier to download English translations of Russian classics than Russian versions, Anatoly Voronov asks, "Why shouldn't Pushkin or Lermontov be more available in Russian

    A) Russian?"   B) Russian"?   C) Russian?".

5) Voronov argues that the need to use English over the Internet divides the world into new sorts of "haves and have-nots

    A) have-nots".   B) have-nots."   C) have-nots"

6) But isn't Christian Huitema, a member of the board of the Internet Society, correct when he says, "The effect of the Internet is to make information available at a minimum cost and effort

    A) effort."   B) effort"?   C) effort?"

7) The need to use English, according to this view, is a small price, indeed, to pay for access to the major libraries of the world

    A) world!   B) world.!   C) world?

8) Another controversy centers on whether or not the Internet should be censored

    A) censored!   B) censored?   C) censored.

9) Web pages are being used not only to provide sexually explicit material and racist propaganda but also to teach people how to make bombs

      A) bombs.   B) bombs?   C) bombs.!

10) The Internet is used by some very dangerous people-con artists, pornographers, sexual predators

      A) predators-   B) predators-.   C) predators.

11) Can the Internet police itself, or do we need protective legislation (such as the proposed Communications Decency Act)

      A) legislation?   B) Decency Act?)   C) Decency Act)?

12) A third controversy centers on who will control the secret codes protecting our most sensitive communications

      A) communications. B) communications? C) communications!

13) To assure the right to absolute privacy, civil libertarians want chips with powerful encryption formulas (formulas that encode communications sent over telephones and computer networks)

      A) formulas. B) networks.) C) networks).

14) To give investigative agencies the means to eavesdrop, the federal government wants the chips to include a "back door key"

      A) key".   B) key."   C) key"

15) One thing is for certain: the Internet has brought with it a host of benefits—and a host of problems

      A) problems. B) problems— C) problems-.

EXERCISE Q: Using Commas

Select the letter of the choice that correctly punctuates the sentence.

1) Elements of mystery and detection, can be found in literature dating as far back as ancient Greece.
    A) detection can   B) literature, dating C) no change

2) In Sophocles' *Oedipus the King*, for instance, Oedipus has to solve a mystery of who killed Laius the former king.
    A) *King*, for instance B) *King*; for instance,   C) Laius, the

3) He goes about his task in a methodical way one that would please any modern detective.
    A) way. One.   B) way, one   C) no change

4) He consults authorities (the Oracle), offers a reward for information, and interrogates witnesses.
    A) authorities, (the   B) Oracle) offers   C) no change

5) And he doesn't stop until he gets his man which is ironic since he is, in fact, the murderer.
    A) man, which is ironic since
    B) man which is ironic, since
    C) man, which is ironic, since

6) Another drama in which the hero plays detective is Shakespeare's *Hamlet*.
    A) drama, in which the hero plays detective, is
    B) drama in which the hero plays detective, is
    C) no change

7) Hamlet is informed by his father's ghost that his Uncle Claudius who now wears the crown has murdered him by pouring poison in the old king's ear while he slept.
    A) ghost, that
    B) Claudius, who now wears the crown, has
    C) no change

8) Thus Hamlet has been told not only who the murderer is but also how the crime was committed.
    A) is, but   B) how, the   C) no change

9) Because Hamlet is not sure the ghost is telling him the truth he comes up with a strategy, one that many detectives in fiction have tried. He sets a trap.

    A) truth, he   B) strategy one   C) no change

10) He has King Claudius watch a play in which a king is murdered under circumstances almost identical to the ones the ghost described and he observes Claudius' reaction.

    A) described, and   B) described and,   C) no change

11) When King Claudius reacts violently to the scene Hamlet is sure he's got his man.

    A) scene, Hamlet   B) sure, he's   C) no change

12) Elements of detective fiction can be found in other great works of literature such as Dostoevsky's *Crime and Punishment* and Victor Hugo's *Les Miserables*.

    A) literature such as,   B) literature,   C) *Punishment*, and

EXERCISE R: Using the Semicolon

Select the letter of the choice that correctly punctuates the sentence.

1) Many people attribute today's high crime rate to social disintegration however the proportion of single, young males appears to be an overlooked factor.

    A) disintegration; however, B) disintegration, however,
    C) disintegration, however;

2) In the nineteenth century, frontier mining towns were populated by single males farming communities were populated by large families.

    A) males, farming   B) males: farming   C) males; farming

3) Mining towns had high murder rates in contrast murders were extremely rare in farming communities.

    A) rates, in contrast, B) rates; in contrast, C) rates, in contrast;

4) For example, the mining town of Bodie, California, averaged 116 murders per 100,000 people Henderson County, Illinois, averaged just 4.3 during the same period.

    A) people, Henderson   B) people; but   C) people; Henderson

5) Immigrants tend to be young and male as a result crime rates are higher in communities with large immigrant populations.

    A) male; as a result, B) male, as a result, C) male; as a result

6) In the 1860s and 1870s, forty-two percent of New York City's homicide victims were Irish immigrants even though they comprised only twenty percent of the city's population.

    A) immigrants. Even though   B) immigrants, even though
    C) immigrants; even though,

7) The behavior of men is most dangerous when they are in their teens and early twenties the years during which they are most likely to commit violent acts like murder.

    A) twenties, the years   B) twenties; the years   C) twenties: the years

8) Some social scientists attribute the violent increase in behavior to the surge of testosterone experienced by boys going through puberty but others attribute it to factors in the social environment.

    A) puberty, but   B) puberty; but   C) puberty; but,

9) These scientists note that men who live with their families have low crime rates men who live alone have high crime rates.

  A) rates; but men B) rates; men   C) rates, men

10) Single men also suffer from high rates of illness and depression on the other hand married men are healthier and happier.

  A) depression, on the other hand

  B) depression; on the other hand,

  C) depression; on the other hand

11) Early in the twentieth century, the life expectancy of a single male was forty-four that of a married man was sixty.

  A) forty-four: that of   B) forty-four, that of C) forty-four; that of

12) Violent crime is common in the inner cities places where young men often grow up without extended families.

  A) cities; places B) cities, places C) cities. Places

13) Family supports young men-by giving them a sense of identity, self-worth, and confidence.

  A) men, by   B) men; by   C) men by

EXERCISE S: Using Apostrophes

Select the letter of the choice that correctly uses apostrophes.

1) One hundred years before Pharaoh Djosers reign, Egypt was a land of small chiefdoms.

      A) Djoser's   B) Djosers'   C) chiefdom's.

2) After his reign, Egypt's civilization was one of the most advanced of it's time.

      A) Egypts'   B) its   C) no change

3) Its the belief of many experts that Djoser created the world's first nation-state.

      A) It's   B) worlds'   C) no change

4) They believe he accomplished this feat by harnessing his countries' manpower to build the Old Kingdom's first great pyramid.

      A) country's   B) Kingdoms'   C) no change

5) The Step Pyramid, royal architect Imhotep's brilliant design, was a marvel of construction.

      A) architect's   B) Imhotep   C) no change

6) Their's was a brilliant but sometimes difficult collaboration.

      A) There's   B) Theirs   C) no change

7) The lives of many generations of ancient Egyptians must've been made grim and tedious by the pharaohs' obsessive preoccupation with immortality.

      A) must have   B) pharaoh's   C) no change

8) Near the pyramids of Giza, workers' graves have been discovered.

      A) pyramid's   B) worker's   C) no change

9) It's evident from their compressed vertebrae and missing fingers and limbs that their's was a hard life.

      A) Its   B) theirs   C) no change

10) However, experts believe that the peoples' faith in their gods rather than the pharaohs' brute force spurred them to complete the enormous projects.

      A) people's   B) pharaoh's   C) no change

11) Hundreds of years later, many of the Old Kingdom's monuments, such as the Sphinx, were'nt even finished.

      A) Kingdoms'   B) weren't   C) no change

12) Perhaps the Egyptian people grew tired of each pharaoh's attempt to build a monument greater than his predecessor.

      A) pharaohs'   B) predecessor's   C) no change

13) The Old Kingdom fell into decay after Pepi I and Pepi II reigns.

      A) Pepi I's and Pepi II's   B) Pepi I and Pepi II's

      C) no change

14) Pepi I, who's reign lasted 34 years, was an aggressive ruler whose armies attacked the lands to the south and west of Egypt.

      A) whose   B) who's   C) no change

15) Pepi II, whose reign lasted 90 years, was'nt an effective ruler.

      A) who's   B) wasn't   C) no change

EXERCISE T: Using Quotation Marks

Select the letter of the choice that correctly punctuates the sentence.

1) Science fiction writer Ursula Le Guin writes: "I was raised as irreligious as a jack rabbit, and probably this is one reason Mark Twain made so much sense to me."

    A) writes "I   B) writes, "I   C) me"

2) She asks, "Could anybody but Mark Twain have told the story of Adam and Eve without mentioning Jehovah."

    A) asks: "Could   B) Jehovah"?   C) Jehovah?"

3) James Joyce's response to complaints about his use of vulgar language is this": This race and this life produced me-I shall express myself as I am."

    A) this, "This   B) this: "This   C) I am".

4) Henry James: The Private Universe is the title of an article written by Graham Greene.

    A) Henry James: "The Private Universe

    B) 'Henry James: The Private Universe'

    C) "Henry James: The Private Universe"

5) Writing about the conclusion of *The Adventures of Huckleberry Finn*, Toni Morrison wonders, "Will that undefined space, so falsely imagined as "open," be free of social chaos, personal morbidity, and further moral complications embedded in adulthood and citizenship?"

    A) 'open'   B) citizenship'?   C) citizenship."?

6) An early view of the novel *Arrowsmith* by Sinclair Lewis concludes with the following assessment: Artistically, *Arrowsmith* is an authentic step forward. The novel is full of passages of a quiet noble felicity and the old skill in presenting character through dialogue never fails. Babbitt is generic or he is nothing (Stewart 36)

    A) Artistically . . . nothing (Stewart 36).

    B) "Artistically . . . nothing." (Stewart 36)

    C) "Artistically . . . nothing" (Stewart 36).

7) Hal Holbrook says that "he wasn't aware of Mark Twain's potential for social commentary until he was in Little Rock in 1957."

    A) until I was

    B) 1957".

    C) No quotation marks needed.

8) In *Roughing It*, Mark Twain has this to say about the fate of the thousands of young men who came to Virginia City seeking gold "all gone, or nearly all-victims devoted upon the altar of the golden calf."

     A) 'Roughing It'   B) gold: "All   C) gold. "All

9) According to an early review of D. H. Lawrence's *Sons and Lovers*, "The book is full of short, vivid descriptions: 'The steep swoop of highroad lay in its cool morning dust...''

     A) "Sons and Lovers"   B) dust...'   C) dust...'"

10) "Art itself," Conrad wrote "may be defined as a single-minded attempt to render the highest kind of justice to the visible universe."

     A) Conrad wrote, "may   B) Conrad wrote. "May
     C) Conrad wrote: "may

11) What a brilliant prediction: "Proust will never be a widely read writer."

     A) 'brilliant'   B) "brilliant"   C) prediction,

12) "Here again is Kipling's old dictum that "East is East and West is West."
     A) 'East is East and West is West.'"
     B) 'East is East and West is West.'
     C) East is East and West is West."

13) According to Donald Adams, Light in August is a powerful novel, a book which secures Mr. Faulkner's place in the very first rank of American fiction writers."

     A) "*Light in August*   B) "'Light in August'   C) "Light in August"

14) Is the following quote about James Joyce's *Ulysses* an elitist remark: "The average intelligent reader will glean little or nothing from it."?

     A) remark, "The   B) from it"?   C) from it?"

EXERCISE U: Using Other Punctuation Marks

Select the letter of the answer that punctuates the sentence most appropriately and correctly.

1) When Percival Lowell an early twentieth-century American astronomer observed Mars through a telescope, he thought he saw a vast network of canals.
    A) [an early twentieth-century American astronomer]
    B) (an early twentieth-century American astronomer)
    C) —an early twentieth-century American astronomer—

2) He hypothesized that Mars had the following features in common with Earth water, vegetation, and, at some time in the past, intelligent life.
    A) Earth; water   B) Earth—water   C) Earth: water

3) The report cited earlier missions only indirectly: "However, three space probes in the 1960s the Mariner missions revealed that Mars had no canals, vegetation, or water."
    A) [the Mariner missions]
    B) (the Mariner missions)
    C) /the Mariner missions/

4) With its distant orbit 140 million miles from the sun and its thin, largely carbon-dioxide atmosphere, Mars has a harsh environment.
    A) no change
    B) (140 million miles from the sun)
    C) ...140 million miles from the sun...

5) The Mariner and later the Viking missions did find evidence that Mars has had a complicated climatic history one punctuated with warm periods.
    A) history—one punctuated with warm periods.
    B) history: one punctuated with warm periods.
    C) history...one

6) Furthermore, researchers have found the other evidence characteristic of glacial landscapes, such as boulder-like ridges of sediment, meandering lines of sand and or gravel, and "rock glaciers," like those found in Alaska.
    A) and-or   B) and/or   C) and, or

7) Researchers have also found long channels emanating from "chaotic terrain" regions of fractured rocks that may have collapsed when groundwater broke suddenly through the surface.
    A) —regions of fractured rocks—
    B) /regions of fractured rocks/
    C) [regions of fractured rock]

8) Once this water rushed to the surface and mixed with the carbon-dioxide in the atmosphere, a carbonated sea a Martian seltzer may have been created.
    A) —a Martian seltzer—   B) (a Martian seltzer)   C) [a Martian seltzer]

9) Some believe Mars may have had more than channels, lakes, and seas there may have been a Martian ocean.
    A) seas (there may have been a Martian ocean).
    B) seas, there
    C) seas: There may have been a Martian ocean.

10) Further evidence of water on Mars comes from Soviet space probes, which revealed oxygen and hydrogen atoms derived from the breakdown of water exposed to sunlight streaming away from Mars.
    A)   [derived from the breakdown of water exposed to sunlight]
    B) —derived from the breakdown of water exposed to sunlight—
    C) sunlight: streaming

11) A quantity of the carbon-dioxide a potent greenhouse gas also appears to have escaped from Mars into space.
    A) "a potent greenhouse gas"   B) —a potent greenhouse gas—
    C) [a potent greenhouse gas]

12) Many questions remain about water on Mars Was there an ocean? When was Mars wet? How long was it wet?
    A) Mars: Was   B) Mars_Was   C) Mars? Was

13) One researcher believes that Mars may have had water on its surface as recently as 300 million years ago a relatively short time in the history of our solar system.
    A) surface: as   B) ago: a relatively   C) ago—a relatively

14) "Recent experiments on Martian meteorites such as the one found in Antarctica raise the possibility that primitive forms of life may have existed on Mars in its distant past."
    A) /such as the one found in Antarctica/
    B) such as, the
    C) [such as the one found in Antarctica]

EXERCISE V: Using Capitalization and Italics

Select the letter of the choice that correctly uses capitalization and/or italics.

1) Charleston, South Carolina, is unique among american cities for its rich history, its plethora of churches, and its beautiful homes.
    A) south carolina   B) American   C) *plethora*   D) no change

2) The site of the city is the peninsula formed by the cooper and ashley rivers, which flow together into the Atlantic.
    A) Peninsula B) Cooper and Ashley Rivers   C) atlantic D) no change

3) At the beginning of the eighteenth century, Charles Towne, as it was then known, was a small, walled city threatened periodically by the Spanish and the Yamassee Indians.
    A) Eighteenth century   B) eighteenth Century
    C) yamassee indians   D) no change

4) While most of the colonists spoke English, French was used by the Huguenots and Spanish by the jews who settled in the city because it offered religious freedom.
    A) English B) huguenots   C) Jews   D) no change

5) Catholics, Protestants, and Jews built so many houses of worship that the city is often called the holy city.
    A) Protestants, and jews   B) Houses of Worship   C) *the holy city*

6) Another tongue often heard in the city was gullah, the language used by African slaves who provided the labor for the outlying rice plantations.
    A) Gullah B) african C) Plantations   D) no change

7) The term gullah refers to the language that resulted from English words being grafted onto African syntax.
    A) *Gullah* B) english C) african D) no change

8) At the beginning of the eighteenth century, the gates of Charleston were located in an area that is now the heart of the downtown, called "the four corners of law" at broad and meeting streets.
    A) Eighteenth Century   B) the four Corners of law
    C) Broad and Meeting   D) no change

9) However, the street that visitors most often ask to see is Cabbage Row, alias *Catfish Row*, the setting for DuBose Heyward's novel Porgy.

    A) cabbage row   B) Catfish Row

    C) *Porgy*   D) no change

10) The Heyward-Washington House, mentioned in DuBose's novel, was once owned by a signer of the declaration of independence; however, it had become a slum by the time it was turned over to the Charleston Museum.

    A) House   B) Declaration of Independence

    C) Charleston museum   D) no change

11) Another frequently visited address, the Villa Margherita at 4 south battery, is where Carol Kennicott, the heroine of Sinclair Lewis's novel *Main Street*, sought refuge from the madness of our modern, materialistic culture.

    A) villa margherita   B) South Battery   C) Main Street   D) no change

12) The Exchange Building, owned by the D.A.R., has been a prison, a customs house, a post office, and a city hall since it was built in 1771.

    A) Exchange building   B) d.a.r.   C) City Hall D) no change

13) The Marine Hospital at 20 Franklin Street was a teaching hospital and a hospital for the confederacy before the Reverend Daniel Jenkins turned it into an orphanage for black children.

    A) 20 Franklin street   B) Confederacy   C) reverend D) no change

14) The college of Charleston, founded in 1785, was the first municipal college in the Northern Hemisphere.

    A) College of Charleston   B) Municipal College

    C) northern hemisphere   D) no change

EXERCISE W: Using Abbreviation and Numbers

Select the letter of the choice that correctly uses numbers and abbreviations.

1) The Endangered Species Act was signed by Pres. Nixon in 1973.
    A) President B) nineteen seventy-three   C) no change

2) In that year, there were 109 names on the list of endangered species.
    A) yr.   B) one hundred and nine   C) no change

3) Now the total is over 900.
    A) tot.   B) nine hundred   C) no change

4) 3,700 of the nation's 150,000 species may qualify for protection.
    A) Three thousand seven hundred
    B) one hundred fifty thousand
    C) Of the nation's 150,000 species, 3,700 may qualify for protection.

5) One-fifth of the 20 thousand plant species in the United States is imperiled.
    A) 1/5   B) twenty thousand C) no change

6) Endangered species range from the 3-inch snail darter to the fifteen-hundred-pound manatee.
    A) three in.   B) three-inch   C) fifteen-hundred lbs.

7) Every branch of the fed gov't., including the Department of Defense, must consult with the wildlife and fish services before proceeding with a project that might harm a species on the threatened or endangered list.
    A) Federal gov't.   B) federal government   C) Dept. of Defense

8) The Endangered Species Act first gained notoriety when it stopped construction of a dam in Tennessee in order to protect the snail darter, which had only recently been discovered by an ichthyologist from the Univ. of Tennessee.
    A) Constr.   B) Tenn.   C) University

9) In the 1980s, the act was used to protect the spotted owl from the logging industry in the Pacific NW.
    A) Pcf.   B) Northwest   C) no change

10) Since the signing of the bill, the number of Calif. gray whales has increased from a few thousand to about 24,000.

    A) no.   B) California   C) 24 thousand

11) Today, breeding pairs of eagles in the 48 states number 4,000.

    A) 48 sts.   B) four thousand   C) no change

12) In a captive breeding program, the red wolf, an eighty lb. predator, has been reintroduced in North Carolina.

    A) eighty-pound   B) N. Carolina   C) no change

13) Loss of habitat is the number one reason why most species are endangered.

    A) # one 1   B) number 1   C) no change

14) Another reason is the 4,500 alien species that have invaded the U.S.

    A) four thousand five hundred   B) United States   C) no change

15) At the current rate of extinction, 1 out of 4 species on the planet will be extinct by the year 2050.

    A) one out of four   B) Twenty-fifty   C) no change

EXERCISE X: Using Hyphens

Select the letter of the choice that correctly uses the hyphen or where a hyphen is unnecessary.

1) The San Andreas Fault emerges full blown beneath Bombay Beach, a fault-laced town of trailers and retirees.

    A) full-blown   B) fault laced   C) no change

2) Some sections of this fault, such as the sixty-mile segment that runs bet-ween Palm Springs and the San Bernardino mountains, seem primed for a quake.

    A) 60 mile   B) be-tween   C) no change

3) Measuring 6.7 on the moment magnitude scale, the Northridge earthquake was the largest one to strike directly under a major U.S. city since the one that struck San Francisco in 1906.

    A) moment-magnitude   B) earth-quake   C) no change

4) The cost of retrofitting the many steel-framed buildings is stagg-ering.

    A) steel framed   B) stag-gering.   C) no change

5) In the next thirty years, California could be rocked by several 30 billion dollar quakes.

    A) thirty-years   B) thirty-billion-dollar   C) no change

6) A large-scale quake could topple many of Los Angeles's high rise complexes.

    A) large scale   B) high-rise   C) no change

7) The whole Los Angeles basin is a 25,000 foot deep sea of sediments that have buried an entire mountain range.

    A) 25,000-foot-deep B) sediments, that   C) no change

8) Locally based geologists have identified more than fifty potential sources for Northridge-size quakes.

    A) Locally-based   B) Northridge size   C) no change

9) Some of the pre-cautions people in the Los Angeles area take against quakes may seem far-fetched to people who haven't experienced a quake.

    A) precautions   B) far fetched   C) no change

10) A screenwriter removed all the bookcases in his home because he feared they might topple-over on him.

     A) screen-writer   B) topple over   C) no change

11) The owner of a winery replaced his sixty-gallon wooden tanks with huge stainless steel drums.

     A) 60 gallon   B) stainless-steel   C) no change

12) An architect built a bed from heavy-duty plywood.

     A) heavy duty   B) ply-wood   C) no change

13) The bed is supported by two inch steel tubing.

     A) two-inch   B) steel-tubing   C) no change

14) Up the coast in San Francisco, engineers are retrofitting the Golden Gate Bridge.

     A) retro-fitting   B) Golden-Gate   C) no change

15) They hope to prevent the collapse of the over-water sections of the world-famous bridge.

     A) over water   B) world famous   C) no change

Answer Keys

For each question in the editing and diagnostic tests and in the exercises, the correct answer, topic tested, and relevant section of the handbooks are identified. The following are the abbreviations used for each handbook:

The Little, Brown Handbook, Brief Edition (LB Brief), Fourth Edition (Aaron): LB

The Longman Handbook for Writers and Readers, Sixth Edition (Anson/Schwegler): LH

The Writer's Handbook for College and Career (Dees/McManus/Schwegler): WH

The New Century Handbook, Fifth Edition (Hult/Huckin): NCH

The Scott, Foresman Handbook for Writers, Ninth Edition (Ruszkiewicz/Friend/Seward/Hairston): SFH

The Scott, Foresman Writer, Fifth Edition (Ruszkiewicz/Seward/Friend/Hairston): SFW

The DK Handbook and *The DK Handbook with Exercises*, Second Edition (Wysocki/Lynch): DK

EDITING TESTS

Editing Test I

1) The waves pounded on the stern of the small green sailboat. (or ; t) Then it rounded the sharp curve in the bay so the wind and current now were flowing together. (or ; t) The two pushed the small craft safely home into its own small inlet.

2) A popular person in our small community is my friend Clara, readily recognized because of her amazing laugh. Its power and infectious delight never cease to captivate me.

3) The middle-aged woman startled all her friends, who gaped in disbelief, as she quit her job, broke off her engagement, and moved halfway across the country to start a new life. Surprisingly, she's happy; (or . S) sometimes rash moves are good ones.

4) Shaney and Tannie seem alike in many ways; (or . B) both earn good grades and have quick, zany senses of humor. Tannie, however, loves sports and the outdoors while Shaney prefers lying on the couch to read novels or to watch videos.

5) John and his friends from high school decided to take a month-long camping trip across the country last August because they all had finished college and were moving to different parts of the country. Amazingly, John's '72 Cutlass made the trip safely.

Editing Test II

1) When my husband Joe had cancer surgery five years ago, each of his family members responded just as I knew he or she would. John, his father, decided to organize the family's calls, because, of course, everything would run so much more smoothly. Thus Jane, Matt, and Jim received detailed sheets of instructions in the mail telling them which days to telephone R. J. Smith Hospital to talk to Joe and what presents to send.

Jane, enraged, promptly threw a tantrum, calling Matt and Jim to complain about her father's overbearing behavior. "I," she yelled, "am a psychiatrist who knows how to handle these situations; (or . I) I am not still a child."

Matt also responded predictably by avoiding the situation. He threw himself into his work. Normally a late sleeper, Matt took to leaving at 5:00 a.m., driving on the deserted expressway, and arriving at work before six a.m. In addition, he didn't return until 11:00 p.m., when he would fall into bed so exhausted that he couldn't worry about Joe.

Jim, too, responded predictably. He fumed inside for weeks, ignored John's instructions, and sent cartons of books to Joe so that he would never be bored. The books were funny because Jim had read Norman Cousins' book about the healing power of laughter. Within a few months, Joe recovered from the surgery—in spite of his family.

Editing Test III

1)   Voice lessons have not met my expectations. I thought Professor Rosman's methods, goals, and repertoire would be predictable and stuffy, not startling and thoroughly unconventional. I knew Rosman's methods were unusual at my first lesson in September of 1990 when he asked me to pretend that I could only make grunts and had no control of my jaw muscles. Another time I had to say "Unique New York" as I sang scales. At one lesson I even had to sing all my songs with "brr" as my only word.

Rosman's goals for me were not, to my relief, to make me sound like an opera singer because I wanted to sound like a torch singer like Linda Ronstadt with the Nelson Riddle Orchestra. Rosman wanted me to enjoy singing, to support my voice with good air flow, and to sing the words as I would speak them. He didn't make me sing opera or art songs, although I did like the Italian and French songs I sang. I sang songs that stretched my voice's range and songs that I liked, songs such as "Can't Help Loving That Man of Mine" and "September Song." My favorites were "The Water Is Wide," a folk song that James Taylor has recorded, and "Amazing Grace," a song that Judy Collins has recorded. Voice lessons have been fun, not what I expected.

Editing Test IV

1) Mary Strong is a librarian who is called Mary Prunella Clapsaddle Jones by her close friends because she collects strange names as other people collect rare stamps. Petite and pretty, she is witty, kind, and startlingly frank.

2) Marian and Matt are lifelong enemies because they are so much alike. She is bright, competitive, and energetic; (or . H) he prides himself on his intellectual ability, his innate superiority, and his persistence. Whenever the two are together, fireworks flare.

3) Marooned on the mud flat, our skiff was useless for the next few hours until the tide came in. We sat on the bank, swatted mosquitoes, and sniped at each other. We were not happy campers.

4) The wind streamed around the tall buildings and roared (or buildings, roaring) down the empty cross-streets. Its force lifted my loose shoe and flung it into the rain-soaked street. I was shocked and shoeless in Chicago.

5) When she was nineteen, she joined the Dolphin Players, which produced quality plays in various small theaters in the city. She remained active in the group until she was twenty-five when she moved to New York City to become a professional actress.

Editing Test V

1)   My first sailing trip taught me two valuable lessons. First, I realized that I always needed to take extra provisions. When we set out, the sky was blue and cloudless, and (or ; or . T) the breeze was warm. We ate our picnic lunch within the first hour. Then we sailed for two more hours, all the way up Shinglehouse Slough. When we headed home, we realized that the tide had already turned and that we had to hurry; (or . H) however, the wind had died. We decided to row. We rowed until we were near Charleston Bridge where the boat snagged on a mud flat. John and I piled out and started to push the boat through the shallow water, hurrying to get to the deeper channel before the tide was completely out. The sun was now gone; (or , and or . F) fog and wind were swirling around the boat. We wanted more food and warmer clothing; (or . B) both were at home, not in the boat.

Then I learned my second lesson: (or ; or . N) nature is powerful. As we reached deeper water, we realized that the waves were growing steadily higher although the fog was beginning to lift. Soon we were surfing on top of the waves in our little skiff, propelled by the wind and the current. I began comparing how far I could swim with how far away the shore was. I sat huddled in the bottom of the boat in an inch of water from the waves' spray. Finally, we nosed the boat into the narrow inlet. We scrambled out. Mother Nature was a tough teacher.

Editing Test VI

1)   When Muriel decided to take up smoking a cigar, she shocked her friends and family; (or . A) also she horrified her husband, Arnold. Because everyone disapproved of her cigar-smoking, Muriel began to avoid her friends, family, and husband. Instead, she started to research the history of cigars; (or . F) furthermore, she began to hang around the local cigar stores on Broadway Avenue. There she met some fascinating people who had knowledge of the wide variety of cigars produced around the world. If Muriel wanted to know about Russian cigars, she asked Josef Asknessazy questions; (or . H) however, if she wanted to understand why Cuban cigars were considered so fine, she asked Juan Canolos.

After she had hung around the cigar shops for months, had read twenty books, and had read the last five years' issues of *Puff*, Muriel felt she knew enough about cigars to defend her habit to anyone. Furthermore, she decided to open her own cigar shop in her neighborhood. Arnold agreed so that he could see more of her. The two opened a small cigar store a few months later. Muriel worked hard, and (or ; or . S) she found a suitable vacant building for the new store. Arnold helped her secure the loan; (or . M) moreover, he was a cosigner. The two cleaned the building, repainted it, and rented the necessary furniture. They now own a thriving business in the heart of Portland. Muriel and Arnold are an American success story.

Editing Test VII

1) The wind howled in the scraggly trees and barren bushes. (or ; t) Then it stopped and the pounding rains started; (or . T) they went on for the next forty hours without diminishing in force.

2) Kate Smith was a famous singer known for her rendition of "God Bless America" and for her propensity for accidents. During the latter years of her life, she broke one leg twice by falling in the same hotel ballroom.

3) Joan and Rich are both characters in different ways: (or ; or .) Joan is totally outrageous in her behavior and will say and do anything, while Rich is witty but not outrageous.

4) Physical injuries can produce innovative adaptations. A good friend who was a professional potter had to give up pottery when her spine was injured because she couldn't apply the pressure necessary to center and hold the clay in place. Now she is a first-rate quilter, showing her work in galleries across the nation.

5) The recent rash of air-traffic controller errors prompted an investigation by the FAA, which found that most errors were a result of pilots and controllers not being able to understand each other's words. The FAA made a startling recommendation: voice training for both groups.

Editing Test VIII

1)   Winifred, my aunt, had a great fondness for "hard cider" as the British call it. She was quite a law-abiding lady with her hair pulled back in a bun and hose with very straight seams, prim in most respects until the aroma of hard cider filled her nostrils. Then she would lift one of her carefully tweezed eyebrows ever so slightly, murmur a vague but polite excuse to those present, and head directly for the cider.
        The family, all of whom knew these alarming symptoms only too well, immediately would launch their individual strategic maneuvers to divert her attention from the cider. Uncle Bob, a man who hated confrontation and who loved mysteries, usually began his own campaign to find the cider source before she found it. Aunt Martha was more direct: (or . S) she would grab Winifred's arm with the force of a well-muscled wrestler and pull her toward the kitchen for a "friendly talk." Uncle John was the cagiest; (or . T) therefore, he was the most successful. With utmost discretion, infinite patience, and resolute determination, he would trail Winifred as if he had no particular interest in where she was going or what she was doing: (or . T) then he would just happen to engage her in a heated conversation on her favorite topic: the Royal Society for the Prevention of Cruelty to Animals.

Because of these strategies, the family managed to keep Winifred's cider consumption to a minimum until that fateful summer of 1979. The swill summer, we called it later.

Editing Test IX

1)   Racquetball is my favorite sport, so I play it two or three times a week except for the weeks of midterms and finals. I play with two boys and one girl. We usually play at the John G. and Jane J. Brown Recreational Center. You have to pay two dollars for the court even if you are a member. Some kids think that's awful, but I think it's fair.

Tuesdays I play with Joe, my neighbor and classmate. He's a wild and crazy guy on the courts. Swinging wildly and forcefully, he hits the ball so hard sometimes that it makes a whistling noise as it zooms past me to smack into the wall. Although we have played racquetball together for two years, I have yet to return one of those killer balls.

My other steady partner is Conrad, a friend who used to play tennis competitively. Conrad plays only for the fun of the game. My own game has improved dramatically since we began playing together a year ago because Conrad encourages me and gives me good tips on how to hit the ball. I've learned how to catch the ball as it comes off the wall and how to serve the ball so that it's almost unreturnable. Last spring I learned the drop and the half-volley shots. Now our games are more fun for both of us.

My other partner, Shirley, is learning to play racquetball, so we just volley for an hour. Although Shirley used to play tennis, she hasn't played for a long time; thus, her game is rusty. Our practice, however, has improved her game. Playing with all three is great fun and great exercise.

DIAGNOSTIC TESTS

DIAGNOSTIC TEST A

1) Answer: A
Topic: Comparative Adjectives
References: LB33c, LH39c, SFW32h, SFH30h, WH37c, NCH30e, DK487

2) Answer: A
Topic: Subject-Verb Agreement
References: LB29d, LH38a–b, SFW33a, SFH22a, WH36b, 39b, NCH29d, DK458

3) Answer: C
Topic: Compound Objects
References: LB19a, LH42, SFW9&35, SFH28a, WH35b, NCH27b–c, DK484

4) Answer: A
Topic: Double Negatives
References: LB33d, LH34j&39d, SFW32g, SFH30g, WH37c, NCHG19, DK243

5) Answer: B
Topic: Possessives
References: LB42a, LH53a, SFW44a, SFH28c, WH56a, NCH50a, DK483, 569

6) Answer: B
Topic: Subject-Verb Agreement
References: LB29f, LH34d&38, SFW33c, SFH22e, WH36b, NCH29e, DK456

7) Answer: C
Topic: Verb Tenses
References: LB26, LH36a–c, SFW34a, SFH23a, WH34a–b, 40a, NCH28b,d, DK461

8) Answer: A
Topic: Pronoun Case
References: LB30, LH37b, SFW35c, SFH28a, WH35b, NCH27c, DK484, DK484

9) Answer: C
Topic: Homonyms
References: LB18b, LH49, SFW8d&45, SFH45b, WH56b, gl, NCHgl–22, DKgl

10) Answer: B
Topic: Adverbs
References: LB33B, LH39a–b, SFW32e–f, SFH30c, WH37b, gl, NCH30d, gl–16, DK498

11) Answer: A
Topic: Pronoun Reference and Antecedent Agreement
References: LB31D, LH38c, SFW35a–b, SFH27c, WH44b, NCH33a, DK473

12) Answer: A
Topic: Confused Words
References: LB25, LH36a, SFW34c, SFH45b, WHgl, NCH45b, DK586

13) Answer: B
Topic: Punctuation
References: LB39–41, LH51-56, SFW38–39, SFH37b, WH54b NCH49a, DK534

14) Answer: D
Topic: Punctuation
References: LB41, LH51–56, SFW39b, SFH37b, WH54b, NCH49b, DK554

15) Answer: B
Topic: Correct Word
References: LB17–19, LH49a, SFW8d&45c, SFH15b, WH52c, NCH41a, DK252

16) Answer: D
Topic: Verb Tenses
References: LB26b, LH36a–c, SFW34a, SFH23a–b, WH34b, NCH28b–e, DK461

17) Answer: C
Topic: Verb Tenses
References: LB26b, LH36, SFW34a, SFH23a, WH34f, NCH28h, DK461

18) Answer: A
Topic: Subject-Verb Agreement
References: LB29j, LH38a–b, SFW33a, SFH22a, WH36b, NCH29b, DK456

19) Answer: B
Topic: Verb Tenses
References: LB26b, LH36, SFW34a, SFH23a–b, WH34b, NCH28b, DK495

20) Answer: A
Topic: Confused Words
References: LB17–19, LH49, SFW8d&45c, SFH45b, WHgl, NCH45b, gl–21, DKgl

21) Answer: A
Topic: Confused Words
References: LB33b, LH49, SFW32e, SFH30c, WH37a–b, gl, NCH30d, gl–16, DK487

22) Answer: C
Topic: Contractions
References: LB42c, LH53b, SFW44a, SFH28c, WH56b, NCH50b, DK569

23) Answer: D
Topic: Capitalization
References: LB47, LH57, SFW43b, SFH41b, WH59b, NCH53b, DK588

24) Answer: B
Topic: Possessives
References: LB42a, LH53a, SFW44a, SFH25b, WH56a, NCH50a–c, DK483

25) Answer: B
Topic: Relative Pronouns
References: LB30c, LH37d, SFW35d, SFH28a, WH35c, gl, NCH27d, gl–22, DK486

26) Answer: C
Topic: Parallel Structure, Wordiness
References: LB16&20, LH46&48, SFW10b&11a, SFH16h&17c, WH48b&50a, NCH36e&38a, DK248&259

27) Answer: C
Topic: Misplaced Modifiers
References: LB34a, LH43a, SFW32a, SFH30a, WH45a, NCH34a, DK474

28) Answer: C
Topic: Passive Voice
References: LB28a, LH36e, SFW34e, SFH23e, WH34d, NCH28g, DK238

29) Answer: A
Topic: Parallel Structure, Wordiness
References: LB16&20, LH46&48, SFW10b&11a, SFH16h&17c, WH48b&50a, NCH36e&38a, DK248&259

30) Answer: D
Topic: Wordiness
References: LB20c, LH48, SFW11a, SFH17c, WH50a, NCH36e, DK259

31) Answer: B
Topic: Wordiness
References: LB20d, LH48, SFW11a, SFH17c, WH50a, NCH36e, DK259

32) Answer: B
Topic: Misplaced Modifiers
References: LB34a, LH43a, SFW32a, SFH30a, WH50a, NCH36e, DK259

33) Answer: B
Topic: Wordiness
References: LB20, LH48, SFW11a, SFH17c, WH50a, NCH36e, DK259
34) Answer: A
Topic: Pronoun Reference, Biased Language
References: LB18&32, LH37&50, SFW8&35a, SFH15d&26b, WH44b&51a, NCH33a&42c, DK472

35) Answer: A
Topic: Restrictive, Non-Restrictive Clauses
References: LB31c, LH51c, SFW9d&38d, SFH29c, WH53d, NCH47j, DK468

36) Answer: B
Topic: Transitions
References: LB40b, LH52, SFW12c, SFH14a, WH54a, NCH48b, DK505

37) Answer: C
Topic: Transitions
References: LB40b, LH52, SFW12c, SFH14a, WH54a, NCH48b, DK505

38) Answer: C
Topic: Semicolon
References: LB40, LH52, SFW39a, SFH37a, WH54a, NCH48b, DK549

39) Answer: E
Topic: Comma Rules
References: LB39, LH51, SFW38, SFH36, WHa–h, NCH47a–j, DK528

40) Answer: C
Topic: Introductory Elements
References: LB39b, LH51b, SFW38, SFH36, WH53b, NCH47a, DK543

41) Answer: D
Topic: Capitalization
References: LB47, LH57, SFW43b, SFH41b, WH59, NCH53b, DK588

42) Answer: E
Topic: Capitalization
References: LB47, LH57, SFW43b, SFH41b, WH59a–c, NCH53a–d, DK588

43) Answer: B
Topic: Fragments
References: LB35, LH40, SFW31a, SFH35a–b, WH42a, NCH31d, DK466

44) Answer: C
Topic: Run-On or Fused
References: LB36, LH34b&41a, SFW11&31, SFH35d, WH43a, NCH32a–d, DK470

45) Answer: B
Topic: Comma Splice
References: LB36, LH41, SFW38, SFH35c, WH43a, NCH32a–d, DK470

46) Answer: A
Topic: Comma Splice
References: LB36, LH41, SFW38, SFH35c, WH43a, NCH32a–d, DK470

47) Answer: A
Topic: Run-On or Fused
References: LB36, LH34b&41a, SFW11&31, SFH35d, WH43a, NCH32a–d, DK470

48) Answer: D
Topic: Fragments
References: LB35, LH40, SFW31a, SFH35a, WH42a, NCH31a–c, DK466

49) Answer: A
Topic: Fragments
References: LB35, LH40, SFW31a, SFH35a, WH42a, NCH31a–c, DK466

50) Answer: C
Topic: Fragments
References: LB35, LH40, SFW31a, SFH35a, WH42a, NCH31a–c, DK466

DIAGNOSTIC TEST B

1) Answer: C
Topic: Confused Words
References: LB25, LH36a, SFW34c, SFH45b, WHgl, NCH45b, DK586,gl

2) Answer: C
Topic: Possessives
References: LB42a, LH53a, SFW44a, SFH28c, WH56a, NCH50d, DK483, 569

3) Answer: B
Topic: Confused Words
References: LB17–19, LH49, SFW8d&45c, SFH45b, WHgl, NCH45b, gl–21, DKgl

4) Answer: B
Topic: Subject-Verb Agreement
References: LB29e, LH38a–b, SFW33a, SFH22e, WH36b, NCH29e, DK456

158

5) Answer: B
Topic: Adjectives and Adverbs
References: LB33b, LH39, SFW9b&32, SFH30c, WH37b, gl, NCH30d, gl–16, DK487

6) Answer: B
Topic: Pronoun Agreement
References: LB30b, LH38c, SFW35b, SFH28a, WH35a, NCH27b, DK473

7) Answer: C
Topic: Verb Tenses
References: LB26b, LH36, SFW34a, SFH23a, WH34b, NCH28b–e, DK461

8) Answer: A
Topic: Comparative Adjectives
References: LB33c, LH39c, SFW32h, SFH30h, WH37c, NCH30e, DK487

9) Answer: C
Topic: Contractions
References: LB42c, LH53b, SFW44a, SFH25b&28c, WH56b, NCH50b, DK569

10) Answer: B
Topic: Subject-Verb Agreement
References: LB29d, LH38a–b, SFW33a, SFH22a, WH36b, 39b, NCH29d, DK458

11) Answer: A
Topic: Verb Tenses
References: LB26b, LH36, SFW34a, SFH23a–b, WH34b, NCH28b–e, DK461

12) Answer: C
Topic: Pronoun Agreement
References: LB31c, LH38c, SFW35b, SFH26b, WH44b, NCH33e, DK473

13) Answer: D
Topic: Punctuation
References: LB39a, LH51–56, SFW38, SFH36a, WH53b, NCH47b, DK542

14) Answer: A
Topic: Verb Tenses
References: LB26a–b, LH36, SFW34a, SFH23a–b, WH40a, NCH28b–e, DK495

15) Answer: B
Topic: Relative Pronouns
References: LB30c, LH37d, SFW35d, SFH28a, WH35c, gl, NCH27d, gl–22, DK486

16) Answer: A
Topic: Confused Words
References: LB17–19, LH49, SFW8d&45c, SFH15b, NCH52c, NCH41a–b, DK252

17) Answer: A
Topic: Verb Tenses
References: LB26a, LH36, SFW34a, SFH23a–b, WH40a, NCH28b–e, DK495

18) Answer: B
Topic: Pronoun Case
References: LB30a, LH37b, SFW35c, SFH28a, WH35b, NCH27c, DK484

19) Answer: B
Topic: Adverbs
References: LB33a, LH39, SFW9b&32e–f, SFH30e, WH37a–b, NCH30c, DK498

20) Answer: A
Topic: Pronoun Agreement
References: LB31d, LH38c, SFW35b, SFH27c, WH44b, NCH33e, DK473

21) Answer: A
Topic: Exact Language
References: LB18b, LH49, SFW8, SFH15b, WH52c, NCH41a–b, DKgl

22) Answer: A
Topic: Confused Words
References: LB32, LH49, SFW35, SHF30h, WH35b, NCH27f, DK487

23) Answer: B
Topic: Possessives
References: LB42a, LH53a, SFW44a, SFH25b, WH56a, NCH50d, DK483

24) Answer: C
Topic: Exact Language
References: LB17–19, LH35, SFW8, SFH15b, WH52c, 64a, NCH45b, DKgl

25) Answer: A
Topic: Double Negatives
References: LB33d, LH34j&39d, SFW32g, SFH30g, WH37c, NCHgl–19, DK243

26) Answer: A
Topic: Pronoun Agreement, Sexist Pronouns
References: LB18&31, LH38c&50c, SFW8&35b, SFH15d&27a, WH44b&51a, NCH33f&DK451&473

27) Answer: C
Topic: Parallel Structure, Misplaced Modifier
References: LB34a, LH43a&46, SFW10b&32a, SFH16h&30a, WH45a&48b, NCH34a&38a, DK474

28) Answer: C
Topic: Misplaced Modifiers
References: LB34a, LH43a, SFW32a, SFH30a, WH45a, NCH34a, DK474

29) Answer: C
Topic: Writing Concisely
References: LB20b–c, LH35, SFW10&11, SFH17c, WH50a, NCH36h, DK253

30) Answer: A
Topic: Writing Concisely
References: LB20b–c, LH35, SFW10&11, SFH17c, WH50a, NCH36h, DK253

31) Answer: B
Topic: Passive Voice, Wordiness
References: LB20c&28a, LH36e&48, SFW11a&34e, SFH17c&23e, WH50a, NCH28g& 36d,e, DK238&259

32) Answer: B
Topic: Misplaced Modifiers
References: LB34a, LH43a, SFW32a, SFH30a, WH45a, NCH34a, DK474

33) Answer: A
Topic: Punctuation
References: LB39&40, LH51–56, SFW38a, SFH36a, WH48b, NCH38f, DK248, DK534

34) Answer: B
Topic: Pronoun Reference, Double Negative
References: LB32&33d, LH34j, SFW32g&35a, SFH26c&30g, WH37c, NCHgl–19, DK243&472

35) Answer: B
Topic: Dangling Modifiers
References: LB34b, LH34e&43b, SFW32a, SFH30a, WH45b, NCH34e, DK474

36) Answer: A
Topic: Transitions
References: LB20f, LH35, SFW12c, SFH14a–b, WH49a, NCH26a, DK505

37) Answer: A
Topic: Transitions
References: LB20f, LH35, SFW12c, SFH14a–b, WH54a, NCH48b, DK505

161

38) Answer: E
Topic: Comma Rules
References: LB39, LH51, SFW38, SFH36a, WH53a–h, NCH47a–c, DK528

39) Answer: B
Topic: Semicolon
References: LB40, LH52, SFW39a, SFH37a, WH54a, NCH48a, DK549

40) Answer: D
Topic: Semicolon
References: LB40, LH52, SFW39a, SFH37a, WH54a, NCH48e, DK549

41) Answer: A
Topic: Capitalization
References: LB47, LH57, SFW43b, SFH41b, WH59b, NCH53b, DK588

42) Answer: E
Topic: Capitalization
References: LB47, LH57, SFW43b, SFH41b, WH59b, NCH53a–d, DK588

43) Answer: D
Topic: Comma Splice
References: LB36, LH41, SFW38, SFH35c, WH43a, NCH32a–d, DK470

44) Answer: C
Topic: Fragments
References: LB35, LH40, SFW31a, SFH35a, WH42a, NCH31a–c, DK466

45) Answer: C
Topic: Comma Splice
References: LB36, LH41, SFW38, SFH35c, WH43a, NCH32a–d, DK470

46) Answer: C
Topic: Comma Splice
References: LB35&36, LH41, SFW38, SFH35c, WH43a, NCH32a–d, DK470

47) Answer: A
Topic: Comma Splice
References: LB36, LH41, SFW38, SFH35c, WH43a, NCH32a–d, DK470

48) Answer: A
Topic: Fragments
References: LB35, LH40, SFW31a, SFH35a, WH42a, NCH31a–c, DK466

49) Answer: D
Topic: Fragments
References: LB35, LH40, SFW31a, SFH35a, WH42a, NCH31a–c, DK466

50) Answer: D
Topic: Comma Splice
References: LB36, LH41, SFW38, SFH35c, WH43a, NCH32a–d, DK470

DIAGNOSTIC TEST C

1) Answer: B
Topic: Comparative Adjectives
References: LB33c, LH39c, SFW32h, SFH30h, WH37c, NCH30e, DK487

2) Answer: A
Topic: Subject-Verb Agreement
References: LB29j, LH38a–b, SFW33d, SFH22a, WH36b, 39b, NCH29e, DK458

3) Answer: B
Topic: Compound Objects
References: LB19a, LH45, SFW35b, SFH28a, WH35b, NCH27b–c, DK484

4) Answer: B
Topic: Double Negatives
References: LB33d, LH34j&39d, SFW32g, SFH30g, WH37c, NCHG19, DK243

5) Answer: C
Topic: Possessives/Confusing Words
References: LB42a, LH53a, SFW44a, SFH25b&28c, WH56a, NCH50d, DK483, 569

6) Answer: A
Topic: Subject-Verb Agreement
References: LB29j, LH38a–b, SFW33a, SFH22a, WH36b, NCH29b, DK456

7) Answer: C
Topic: Verb Tenses
References: LB26, LH36, SFW34a, SFH23a–b, WH34b, 40a, NCH28b–e, DK461

8) Answer: A
Topic: Pronoun Case
References: LB30d, LH37b, SFW35c, SFH28a, WH35b, NCH27c, DK484

9) Answer: B
Topic: Pronoun Agreement
References: LB31c, LH38c, SFW35b, SFH27a, WH44b, NCH39e, DK473

10) Answer: B
Topic: Adverbs
References: LB33b, LH39, SFW9b&32e–f, SFH30c, WH37a, NCH30d, DK498

11) Answer: A
Topic: Confused Words
References: LB17–19, LH49, SFW8d&45c, SFH15b, WH52c, NCH41a–b, gl-19, DK253

12) Answer: C
Topic: Confused Words
References: LB17–19, LH49, SFW8d&45c, SFHgl, WHgl, NCH45b, gl–17, DKgl

13) Answer: B
Topic: Verb Tenses
References: LB26, LH36, SFW34a, SFH23a–b, WH34f, NCH28h, DK461

14) Answer: A
Topic: Confused Words
References: LB17–19, LH49, SFW8d&45c, SFHgl, WHgl, NCHgl–20, DKgl

15) Answer: A
Topic: Confused Words
References: LB17–19, LH49, SFW8d&45c, SFHgl, WHgl, NCH45b, gl–21, DKgl

16) Answer: B
Topic: Subjunctive
References: LB27a, LH36g, SFW34f, SFH23f, WH34f, NCH28h, DK493

17) Answer: C
Topic: Verb Tenses
References: LB26, LH36, SFW34a, SFH23a–b, WH40a, NCH28b–e, DK495

18) Answer: A
Topic: Subject-Verb Agreement
References: LB29g, LH38a–b, SFW33d, SFH27e, WH36b, NCH29e, DK456

19) Answer: C
Topic: Punctuation
References: LB41, LH51–56, SFW39b, SFH37b, WH54b, NCH49a, DK550

20) Answer: A
Topic: Subject-Verb Agreement
References: LB29g, LH38a–b, SFW33a, SFH22a, WH36b, NCH29e, DK456

21) Answer: B
Topic: Confused Words
References: LB33b, LH49, SFW32e, SFH30c, WH37b, gl, NCH30d, gl–16, DK498

22) Answer: C
Topic: Possessives
References: LB42a, LH53a, SFW44a, SFH25b, WH56a, NCH50c, DK483

23) Answer: B
Topic: Pronoun Case
References: LB30c, LH37d, SFW35c, SFH28a, WH35c, gl, NCH27d, gl–22, DK486

24) Answer: D
Topic: Pronoun Case and Antecedent Agreement
References: LB31d, LH37b&38c, SFW35c, SFH27c, WH35a, NCH27e, DK484

25) Answer: B
Topic: Demonstrative Pronouns
References: LB32, LH37b, SFW35, SFH26, WH44b, NCH26a, DK485

26) Answer: B
Topic: Misplaced Modifiers
References: LB34a, LH43a, SFW32a, SFH30a, WH45a, NCH34a, DK474

27) Answer: C
Topic: Wordiness, Passive Voice
References: LB20b&28a, LH36e, SFW11a&34e, SFH17c&23e, WH34d, 50a, NCH28g, 36d,e, DK238, 259

28) Answer: D
Topic: Wordiness, Parallel Structure
References: LB20, LH46&48, SFW10b&11a, SFH16h&17c, WH48b, 50a, NCH36e, 38a, DK248, 259

29) Answer: C
Topic: Wordiness, Parallel Structure
References: LB16&20, LH46&48, SFW10b&11a, SFH16h&17c, WH48b, 50a, NCH36e, 38a, DK248, 259

30) Answer: D
Topic: Wordiness
References: LB20b–c,g, LH48, SFW11a, SFH17c, WH50a, NCH36e, DK259

31) Answer: B
Topic: Wordiness
References: LB20b, LH48, SFW11a, SFH17c, WH50a, NCH36e, DK259

32) Answer: C
Topic: Wordiness
References: LB20, LH48, SFW11a, SFH17c, WH50a, NCH36e, DK259

33) Answer: D
Topic: Misplaced Modifiers
References: LB34a, LH43a, SFW32a, SFH30a, WH45a, NCH34a, DK474

34) Answer: A
Topic: Pronoun Reference, Biased Language
References: LB32a, LH42&50, SFW8&35a, SFH15d&26b, WH44b, 51a–b NCH33e, DK451, 472

35) Answer: C
Topic: Parallel Structure
References: LB17b, LH46, SFW10b, SFH16h, WH48b, NCH38a, DK248

36) Answer: B
Topic: Transitions
References: LB40b, LH51&52, SFW12c, SFH14a, WH54a, NCH48b, DK505

37) Answer: C
Topic: Transitions
References: LB40b, LH51&52, SFW12c, SFH14a, WH54a, NCH48b, DK505

38) Answer: B
Topic: Comma Rules
References: LB39a–c, LH51, SFW38, SFH36d, WH53a–h, NCH47j, DK528

39) Answer: D
Topic: Comma Rules
References: LB39, LH51, SFW38, SFH36, WH53a–h, NCH47b, DK528

40) Answer: E
Topic: Punctuation
References: LB39g, LH51–56, SFW37–38,40, SFH36, WH53b&57a, NCH47a&49a–b, DK528

41) Answer: D
Topic: Capitalization
References: LB47, LH57, SFW43b, SFH41b, WH59b, NCH53b, DK588

42) Answer: E
Topic: Capitalization
References: LB47, LH57, SFW43b, SFH41b, WH59a–c, NCH53a–d, DK588

43) Answer: A
Topic: Fragments
References: LB35&36, LH40, SFW31a, SFH35a, WH42a, NCH31a–d, DK466

44) Answer: C
Topic: Run-On or Fused
References: LB36, LH34b&41a, SFW11&31, SFH35d, WH43a, NCH32a–d, DK470

45) Answer: D
Topic: Fragments
References: LB35&36, LH40, SFW31a, SFH35a, WH43a, NCH31a–c, DK466

46) Answer: A
Topic: Comma Splice
References: LB36, LH41, SFW38, SFH35c, WH43a, NCH32a–d, DK470

47) Answer: C
Topic: Run-On or Fused
References: LB36, LH34b&41a, SFW11&31, SFH35d, WH43a, NCH32a–d, DK470

48) Answer: B
Topic: Comma Splice
References: LB36, LH41, SFW38, SFH35c, WH43a, NCH32a–d, DK470

49) Answer: B
Topic: Fragments
References: LB35, LH40, SFW31a, SFH35a, WH4a, NCH31a–c, DK470

50) Answer: D
Topic: Comma Splice
References: LB36, LH41, SFW38, SFH35c, WH43a, NCH32a–d, DK470

DIAGNOSTIC TEST D

1) Answer: B
Topic: Confused Words
References: LB17–19, LH49, SFW8d&45c, SFHgl, WHgl, NCH45b, gl–15, DKgl

2) Answer: B
Topic: Confused Words
References: LB33b, LH49, SFW32e, SFH30c, WH37b, gl, NCH30d, gl–16, DK498

3) Answer: C
Topic: Contractions
References: LB42c, LH53b, SFW44a, SFH28c, WH56b, gl, NCHgl–22, DK569

4) Answer: B
Topic: Confused Words
References: LB33b, LH49, SFW35, SFHgl, WH56b, gl, NCHgl–22, DK586

5) Answer: B
Topic: Relative Pronouns
References: LB30d, LH37, SFW35d, SFH28c, WH35a–b, NCH, DK486

6) Answer: B
Topic: Confused Words
References: LB17–19, LH49, SFW8d&45c, SFHgl, WH64a, NCH45b, DK586

7) Answer: B
Topic: Contractions
References: LB42c, LH53b, SFW44a, SFH28c, WH56b, NCH50b, DK569

8) Answer: A
Topic: Confused Words
References: LB17–19, LH49, SFW8d&45c, SFHgl, WHgl, gl–17, DKgl

9) Answer: B
Topic: Subjunctive
References: LB27a, LH36g, SFW34f, SFH23f, WH34f, NCH28h, DK493

10) Answer: A
Topic: Subject-Verb Agreement
References: LB29d, LH38a–b, SFW33a, SFH22a, WH36b, 39b, NCH29d, DK458

11) Answer: A
Topic: Pronoun Reference and Antecedent Agreement
References: LB32b, LH42, SFW35a–b, SFH22b, WH44b, NCH33e, DK472

12) Answer: A
Topic: Verb Tenses
References: LB26, LH36, SFW34a, SFH23a–b, WH40a, NCH28b–e, DK495

13) Answer: B
Topic: Verb Tenses
References: LB26, LH36, SFW34a, SFH23a–b, WH40a, NCH28b–e, DK495

14) Answer: A
Topic: Verb Tenses
References: LB26, LH36, SFW34a, SFH23a–b, WH40a, NCH28b–e, DK461

15) Answer: B
Topic: Possessives
References: LB42a, LH53a, SFW44a, SFH25b, WH56a, NCH50a, DK483

16) Answer: B
Topic: Comma Rules
References: LB39d, LH51, SFW38, SFH6a, WH53e, NCH47c, DK528

17) Answer: B
Topic: Parallel Structure
References: LB16d, LH46, SFW10b, SFH23e, WH48b, NCH38a, DK248

18) Answer: B
Topic: Pronoun Case
References: LB30c, LH37d, SFW35c, SFH28a, WH35c, gl, NCH27d, gl–22, DK486

19) Answer: B
Topic: Contractions
References: LB42c, LH53b, SFW44a, SHF44a, WH56b, NCH50b, DK569

20) Answer: A
Topic: Confused Words
References: LB17–19, LH49, SFW8d&45c, SFHgl, WH64a, NCH45a–b, DK586, DKgl

21) Answer: B
Topic: Confused Words
References: LB17–19, LH49, SFW8d&45c, SFHgl, WHgl, NCH45b, gl–15, DK586

22) Answer: A
Topic: Parallel Structure
References: LB16d, LH46, SFW10b, SFH16h, WH48b, NCH38a, DK248

23) Answer: B
Topic: Possessives
References: LB42a, LH53a, SFW44a, SFH25b, WH56a, NCH50a, DK483

24) Answer: A
Topic: Confused Words
References: LB33b, LH49, SFW32e, SFH30c, WH37b, gl, NCH30d, gl–16, DK487

25) Answer: A
Topic: Confused Words
References: LB17–19, LH49, SFW34c, SFHgl, WH34c, gl, NCH28f, gl–20, , DK586

26) Answer: C
Topic: Pronoun Agreement
References: LB31&32, LH38c, SFW35b, SFH28b, WH44b, NCH39e, DK473

27) Answer: D
Topic: Subject-Verb Agreement
References: LB29d, LH38a–b, SFW33, SFH22a, WH36b, 39b, NCH29d, DK458

28) Answer: C
Topic: Indirect Quotations
References: LB43e, LH44d&54, SFW40a, SFH38, WH57a, NCH51a, DK533

29) Answer: C
Topic: Punctuation
References: LB39&40, LH51–56, SFW39b, SFH37a–b, WH54a–b, NCH48c, 49a, DK549, 550

30) Answer: B
Topic: Coordination/Subordination
References: LB15c–d, LH47, SFW9e–f, SFH16f, WH53c, NCH37a–c, DK246

31) Answer: D
Topic: Fragments
References: LB35, LH40, SFW31a, SFH35a, WH4a, NCH31a–c, DK466

32) Answer: D
Topic: Wordiness, Misplaced Modifier
References: LB20, LH43a&48, SFW11a&32a, SFH17c&30a, WH45a&50a, NCH36e&34a, DK474

33) Answer: D
Topic: Confused Words
References: LB25, LH49, SFW34c, SHF23b&gl, WH34c&gl, NCH28f, gl–20, DK586, DKgl

34) Answer: C
Topic: Misplaced Modifiers
References: LB34a, LH43a, SFW32a, SFH30a, WH45a, NCH34a, DK474

35) Answer: D
Topic: Writing Concisely
References: LB20, LH45, SFW10&11, SFH17c, WH50a–c, NCH36e, DK259

170

36) Answer: A
Topic: Compound Sentences, Adverbial Conjunctions
References: LB19a, LH35c&52, SFW10&32f, SFH14a, WH54a, NCH48b, DK505

37) Answer: C
Topic: Compound Sentences, Adverbial Conjunctions
References: LB19a, LH35c&52, SFW10&32f, SFH14a, WH54a, NCH48b, DK505

38) Answer: A
Topic: Semicolon
References: LB40b, LH52, SFW39a, SFH37a, WH54a, NCH48b, DK549

39) Answer: B
Topic: Semicolon
References: LB40b, LH52, SFW39a, SFH37a, WH54a, NCH48a, DK549

40) Answer: A
Topic: Introductory Elements and Fragments
References: LB35&39b, LH40&51b, SFW31a&38b, SFH36a&36c, WH4a, NCH31a–c& 47a, DK549

41) Answer: D
Topic: Capitalization
References: LB47, LH57, SFW43b, SFH41b, WH59b, NCHa–d, DK588

42) Answer: E
Topic: Capitalization
References: LB47, LH57, SFW43b, SFH41b, WH59a–c, NCH53a–d, DK588

43) Answer: B
Topic: Fragments
References: LB35, LH40, SFW31a, SFH35a, WH4a, NCH31a–d, DK466

44) Answer: A
Topic: Fragments
References: LB35, LH40, SFW31a, SFH35a, WH4a, NCH31a–c, DK466

45) Answer: D
Topic: Run-On or Fused
References: LB36, LH34b&41a, SFW11&31, SFH35d, WH43a, NCH32a–d, DK470

46) Answer: C
Topic: Comma Splice
References: LB36, LH41, SFW38, SFH35c, WH43a, NCH32a–d, DK470

47) Answer: A
Topic: Comma Splice
References: LB36, LH41, SFW38, SFH35c, WH43a, NCH32a–d, DK470

48) Answer: B
Topic: Fragments
References: LB35, LH40, SFW31a, SFH35a, WH42a, NCH31a–c, DK466

49) Answer: B
Topic: Fragments
References: LB35, LH40, SFW31a, SFH35a, WH42a, NCH31a–c, DK466

50) Answer: D
Topic: Comma Splice
References: LB36, LH41, SFW38, SFH35c, WH43a, NCH32a–d, DK470

DIAGNOSTIC TEST E

1) Answer: A
Topic: Confused Words
References: LB17–19, LH49, SFW8d&45c, SFHgl, WHgl, NCH45b&gl–21, DKgl

2) Answer: B
Topic: Confused Words
References: LB17–19, LH49, SFW45c, SFHgl, WH56b&gl, NCHgl–22, DK586

3) Answer: A
Topic: Confused Words
References: LB17–19, LH49, SFW8d&45c, SFHgl, WHgl, NCH45b, gl–15, DK586

4) Answer: A
Topic: Pronoun Agreement and Misuse of Apostrophes
References: LB31d, LH38c&53, SFW35b&44a, SFH28c, WH56a–b, NCH33e, 50d, DK569

5) Answer: A
Topic: Confused Words
References: LB33b, LH49, SFW32e, SFH30c, WH37b&gl, NCH30d, gl–16, DK487

6) Answer: D
Topic: Pronoun Case
References: LB30a–b, LH37b, SFW35c, SFH28a, WH35b, NCH27c, DK484

7) Answer: A
Topic: Contractions
References: LB42c, LH53b, SFW44a, SFH28c, WHgl, NCH45b, DKgl

8) Answer: B
Topic: Contractions
References: LB42c, LH53b, SFW44a, SFH28c, WH56b, NCH50b&gl–23, DK569

9) Answer: C
Topic: Contractions
References: LB42c, LH53b, SFW44a, SFH28c, WH56b, gl, NCH50b&gl–22, DK569

10) Answer: A
Topic: Pronoun Case
References: LB30a, LH37b, SFW35c, SFH28a, WH35b, NCH27c, DK484

11) Answer: B
Topic: Relative Pronouns
References: LB30c, LH37d, SFW35d, SFH28a, WH35c&gl, NCH27d&gl–23, DK486

12) Answer: A
Topic: Capitalization
References: LB47, LH57, SFW43b, SFH41b, WH59b, NCH53b, DK588

13) Answer: B
Topic: Possessives
References: LB42a, LH53a, SFW44a, SFH25b, WH56a, NCH50a, DK483

14) Answer: C
Topic: Verb Tenses
References: LB26b–c, LH36, SFW34a, SFH23a, WH34e, 40a, NCH28b–e, DK461

15) Answer: B
Topic: Subject-Verb Agreement
References: LB29, LH38a–b, SFW33d, SFH22e, WH36b, NCH29e, DK459

16) Answer: A
Topic: Homonyms
References: LB18b, LH49, SFW8d&45, SFHgl, WHgl, NCH45b&gl–21, DKgl

17) Answer: B
Topic: Subject-Verb Agreement
References: LB29, LH38a–b, SFW33d, SFH22a, WH36b, NCH29e, DK459

18) Answer: B
Topic: Confused Words
References: LB17–19, LH49, SFW8d&45c, SFHgl, WHgl, NCHgl–18, DKgl

19) Answer: A
Topic: Confused Words
References: LB17–19, LH49, SFW8d&45c, SFHgl, WH52c, NCH41a–b&gl–19, DK253

20) Answer: B
Topic: Subject-Verb Agreement
References: LB29, LH38a–b, SFW33a, SFH22a, WH36b, NCH29e, DK456

21) Answer: A
Topic: Colon
References: LB41a, LH52b, SFW39b, SFH37b, WH54b, NCH49a, DK554

22) Answer: A
Topic: Plurals
References: LB42b, SFW44a, SFH25a, WH64a, NCH50d, DK483

23) Answer: C
Topic: Verb Tenses
References: LB26b, LH36, SFW34a, SFH23a, WH34b, 40a, NCH28b–e, DK461

24) Answer: D
Topic: Colon
References: LB41a, LH52b, SFW39b, SFH37b, WH54b, NCH49a, DK554

25) Answer: A
Topic: Confused Words
References: LB17–19, LH49, SFW8d&45c, SFHgl, WHgl, NCHgl–18, DKgl

26) Answer: C
Topic: Apostrophes, Possession
References: LB42a, LH53a, SFW44a, SFH28b, WH56a, NCH50d, DK483

27) Answer: D
Topic: Subject-Verb Agreement
References: LB26d, LH38a–b, SFW33a, SFH22a, WH36b, 39b, NCH29d, DK458

28) Answer: A
Topic: Indirect Quotations
References: LB43e, LH44d&54, SFW40a, SFH38, WH57a, NCH51a, DK533

29) Answer: D
Topic: Fragments
References: LB35, LH40, SFW31a, SFH35a, WH42a, NCH31a–c, DK466

30) Answer: D
Topic: Colon
References: LB41a, LH52b, SFW39b, SFH37b, WH54b, NCH49a, DK554

31) Answer: C
Topic: Double Negatives
References: LB33d, LH34j&39d, SFW32g, SFH30g, WH37c, NCHgl–19, DK243

32) Answer: B
Topic: Subject-Verb Agreement
References: LB29, LH38a–b, SFW33a, SFH22a, WH36b, NCH29c, DK458

33) Answer: B
Topic: Quotation Marks
References: LB43a, LH54, SFW40a, SFH38a, WH57c, NCH51a, DK533

34) Answer: C
Topic: Parallel Structure
References: LB17b, LH46, SFW10b, SFH16h, WH48b, NCH38a, DK248

35) Answer: C
Topic: Parallel Structure
References: LB17b, LH46, SFW10b, SFH16h, WH48b, NCH38a, DK248

36) Answer: C
Topic: Transitions
References: LB19, LH35&52, SFW12c, SFH14a, WH54a, NCH48b, DK505

37) Answer: D
Topic: Transitions
References: LB19, LH35&52, SFW12c, SFH14a, WH54a, NCH48b, DK505

38) Answer: D
Topic: Comma Rules
References: LB39f, LH51, SFW38, SFH36, WH53a–h, NCH47j, DK528

39) Answer: B
Topic: Comma Rules
References: LB39, LH51, SFW38, SFH36, WH53a–h, NCH47j, DK528

40) Answer: E
Topic: Comma Rules
References: LB39a, LH51, SFW38 SFH36, WH53a–h, NCH47j, DK528

41) Answer: E
Topic: Capitalization
References: LB47, LH57, SFW43b, SFH41b, WH59c, NCH53a–c, DK588

42) Answer: A
Topic: Capitalization
References: LB47, LH57, SFW43b, SFH41b, WH59c, NCH53b, DK588

43) Answer: A
Topic: Run-On or Fused
References: LB37, LH34b&41a, SFW11&31, SFH35d, WH43a, NCH32a–d, DK470

44) Answer: B
Topic: Fragments
References: LB35, LH40, SFW31a, SFH35a, WH42a, NCH31a–c, DK466

45) Answer: B
Topic: Run-On or Fused
References: LB36, LH34b&41a, SFW11&31, SFH35d, WH43a, NCH32a–d, DK470

46) Answer: C
Topic: Comma Splice
References: LB36, LH41, SFW38, SFH35c, WH43a, NCH32a–d, DK470

47) Answer: A
Topic: Fragments
References: LB35, LH40, SFW31a, SFH35a, WH42a, NCH31a–c, DK466

48) Answer: D
Topic: Fragments
References: LB35, LH40, SFW31a, SFH35a, WH42a, NCH31a–c, DK466

49) Answer: C
Topic: Fragments
References: LB35, LH40, SFW31a, SFH35a, WH42a, NCH31a–c, DK466

50) Answer: A
Topic: Run-On or Fused
References: LB36, LH34b&41a, SFW11&31, SFH35d, WH43a, NCH32a–d, DK470

DIAGNOSTIC TEST F

1) Answer: A
Topic: Pronoun Case
References: LB30a, LH37b, SFW35c, SFH28a, WH35b, NCH27f, DK487

2) Answer: B
Topic: Contractions
References: LB42c, LH53b, SFW44a, SFH28c, 56b&gl, NCH50b&gl–20, DK569

3) Answer: C
Topic: Capitalization
References: LB47, LH57, SFW43b, SFH41b, WH59b, NCH53b, DK588

4) Answer: D
Topic: Possessives
References: LB42a, LH53a, SFW44a, SFH25b, WH56a, NCH5050c, DK483

5) Answer: A
Topic: Confused Words
References: LB17–19, LH49, SFW8d&45c, SFHgl, WHgl, NCH45b, gl–21, DKgl

6) Answer: C
Topic: Verb Tenses
References: LB26b, LH36, SFW34a, SFH32a, WH34b, 40a, NCH28b–e, DK461

7) Answer: C
Topic: Verb Tenses
References: LB26b, LH36, SFW34a, SFH32a, WH34b, 40a, NCH28b–e, DK461

8) Answer: B
Topic: Pronoun Case
References: LB30a–b, LH37b, SFW35c, SFH28a, WH35b, NCH27c, DK486

9) Answer: A
Topic: Subject-Verb Agreement
References: LB29, LH38a–b, SFW33d, SFH22e, WH36b, NCH29e, DK458

10) Answer: A
Topic: Confused Words
References: LB17–19, LH49, SFW8d&45c, SFHgl, WH52c, NCH41a–b, gl–19, DK253

11) Answer: B
Topic: Confused Words
References: LB17–19, LH49, SFW8d&45c, SFHgl, WH52c, gl, NCH41a–b, gl–15, DKgl

177

12) Answer: B
Topic: Colon
References: LB41b, LH52b, SFW39b, SFH37b, WH54b, NCH49a, DK554

13) Answer: D
Topic: Punctuation
References: LB39h, LH51–56, SFW38d, SFH37b, WH54b, NCH49a, DK526

14) Answer: A
Topic: Confused Words
References: LB17–19, LH49, SFW34c, SFHgl, WHgl, NCH45b, DKgl

15) Answer: D
Topic: Pronoun Agreement
References: LB31d, LH38c, SFW35b, SFH27c, WH44b, NCH33e, DK473

16) Answer: B
Topic: Confused Words
References: LB45, LH49, SFW8d&45c, SFHgl, WHgl, NCHgl–22, DKgl

17) Answer: A
Topic: Contractions
References: LB42c, LH53b, SFW44a, SFH28c, WH56b, gl, NCH50b, gl–22, DK569

18) Answer: B
Topic: Pronoun Case
References: LB30b, LH37b, SFW35c, SFH28a–b, WH35a, NCH27e, DK486

19) Answer: B
Topic: Verb Tenses
References: LB26a–b, LH36, SFW34a, SFH32a, WH34e, NCH28b–e, DK461

20) Answer: A
Topic: Subject-Verb Agreement
References: LB29, LH38a–b, SFW33c, SFH22e, WH36b, NCH29e, DK456

21) Answer: A
Topic: Double Negatives
References: LB33d, LH34j&39d, SFW32g, SFH30g, WH37c, NCHG19, DK243

22) Answer: A
Topic: Possessives
References: LB42a, LH53a, SFW44a, SFH28c, WH56a, NCH50d, DK483, 569

23) Answer: B
Topic: Subject-Verb Agreement
References: LB29, LH38a–b, SFW33d, SFH22a, WH36b, 39b, NCH29d, DK458

24) Answer: B
Topic: Comparative Adjectives
References: LB33c, LH39c, SFW32h, SFH30h, WH37c, NCH30e, DK487

25) Answer: B
Topic: Confused Words
References: LB42c, LH49 apostrophe, SFW44a, SFH28c,gl, WHgl, NCHgl–23, DKgl

26) Answer: B
Topic: Relative Clause
References: LB30c, LH37d, SFW9d, SFH35a, WH35c, gl, NCH27d, gl–22, DK486

27) Answer: C
Topic: Parallel Structure
References: LB16, LH46, SFW10b, SFH16h, WH48b, NCH38a, DK248

28) Answer: D
Topic: Parallel Structure
References: LB16, LH46, SFW10b, SFH16h, WH48b, NCH38a, DK248

29) Answer: A
Topic: Subject-Verb Agreement, Parenthetical Expressions
References: LB29&56a, LH38&51d, SFW33, SFH36b, WH36b, NCH29d, DK453, 548

30) Answer: A
Topic: Absolute Phrase
References: LB40, LH43d, SFW9c, SFH16c, WH33c, NCH26c, DK528

31) Answer: C
Topic: Parallel Structure
References: LB16d, LH46, SFW10b, SFH16h, WH48b, NCH38a, DK248

32) Answer: B
Topic: Quotation Marks
References: LB43a, LH54, SFW40a, SFH38a, WH57a, NCH51a, DK570

33) Answer: D
Topic: Wordiness
References: LB17a, LH48, SFW11a, SFH17c, WH50a, NCH36e, DK259

34) Answer: C
Topic: Wordiness
References: LB20d, LH48, SFW11a, SFH17c, WH50a, NCH36e, DK259

35) Answer: D
Topic: Wordiness
References: LB20d, LH48, SFW11a, SFH37c, WH50a, NCH36e, DK259

36) Answer: A
Topic: Transitions
References: LB40b, LH35&52, SFW12c, SFH14a, WH54a, NCH48b, DK505

37) Answer: D
Topic: Transitions
References: LB40b, LH35&52, SFW12c, SFH14a, WH54a, NCH48b, DK505

38) Answer: E
Topic: Comma Rules
References: LB39, LH51, SFW38, SFH36, WH53a–h, NCH47a-h, DK528

39) Answer: D
Topic: Semicolon
References: LB40, LH52, SFW39a, SFH37a, WH54a, NCH48a–e, DK549

40) Answer: B
Topic: Comma Rules
References: LB39, LH51, SFW38, SFH36, WH54a–h, NCH47a-h, DK528

41) Answer: E
Topic: Capitalization
References: LB47, LH57, SFW43b, SFH41b, WH59a–b, NCH53a–c, DK588

42) Answer: D
Topic: Capitalization
References: LB47, LH57, SFW43b, SFH41b, WH59a–b, NCH53a–c, DK588

43) Answer: C
Topic: Comma Splice
References: LB36, LH41, SFW38, SFH35c, WH43a, NCH32a–d, DK470

44) Answer: D
Topic: Fragments
References: LB35, LH40, SFW31a, SFH35a, WH42a–c, NCH31a–c, DK466

45) Answer: C
Topic: Fragments
References: LB35, LH40, SFW31a, SFH35a, WH42a–c, NCH31a–c, DK466

46) Answer: A
Topic: Fragments
References: LB35, LH40, SFW31a, SFH35a, WH42a, NCH31a–c, DK466

47) Answer: C
Topic: Fragments
References: LB35, LH40, SFW31a, SFH35a, WH42a, NCH31a–c, DK466

48) Answer: A
Topic: Comma Splice
References: LB36, LH41, SFW38, SFH35c, WH43a–b, NCH32a–d, DK470

49) Answer: B
Topic: Comma Splice
References: LB36, LH41, SFW38, SFH35c, WH43a–b, NCH32a–d, DK470

50) Answer: C
Topic: Fragments
References: LB35, LH40, SFW31a, SFH35a, WH42a, NCH31a–c, DK466

DIAGNOSTIC TEST G

1) Answer: C
Topic: Wordiness/Redundancies/Conciseness
References: LB20b, LH48, SFW8&11, SFH17b–c, WH50a–c, NCH36e, DK259

2) Answer: B
Topic: Wordiness/Redundancies/Conciseness
References: LB20c, LH48, SFW8&11, SFH17b–c, WH50a–c, NCH36a–b,h, DK259

3) Answer: D
Topic: Wordiness/Conciseness
References: LB20d, LH48, SFW8&11, SFH17b–c, WH50a–c, NCH36h, DK259

4) Answer: B
Topic: Denotation/Connotation
References: LB17–19, LH49, SFW8d, SFH15b, WH52c, NCH41a–b, DK253

5) Answer: A
Topic: Denotation/Connotation
References: LB17–19, LH49, SFW8d, SFH15b, WH52c, NCH41a–b, DK253

6) Answer: A
Topic: Denotation/Connotation
References: LB18b, LH49, SFW8d, SFH15b, WH52c, NCH41a–b, DK253

7) Answer: C
Topic: Dangling Modifiers
References: LB34b, LH34e&43b, SFW32a, SFH30a, WH45b, NCH34e, DK474

8) Answer: D
Topic: Dangling Modifiers
References: LB34b, LH34e&43b, SFW32a, SFH30a, WH45b, NCH34e, DK474

9) Answer: B
Topic: Dangling Modifiers
References: LB34b, LH34e&43b, SFW32a, SFH30a, WH45b, NCH34e, DK474

10) Answer: A
Topic: Dangling Modifiers
References: LB34b, LH34e&43b, SFW32a, SFH30a, WH45b, NCH34e, DK474

11) Answer: C
Topic: Coordination/Subordination
References: LB15c–d, LH47, SFW9e–f, SFH16f, WH49a–c, NCH37a–c, DK246

12) Answer: C
Topic: Coordination/Subordination
References: LB15c–d, LH47, SFW9e–f, SFH16f, WH49a–c, NCH37a–c, DK246

13) Answer: C
Topic: Coordination/Subordination
References: LB15c–d, LH47, SFW9e–f, SFH16f, WH49a–c, NCH37a–c, DK246

14) Answer: B
Topic: Coordination/Subordination
References: LB15c–d, LH47, SFW9e–f, SFH16f, WH49a–c, NCH37a–c, DK246

15) Answer: C
Topic: Parallelism
References: LB16, LH46, SFW10b, SFH16h, WH48b, NCH38a, DK248

16) Answer: B
Topic: Parallelism
References: LB16, LH46, SFW10b, SFH16h, WH48b, NCH38a, DK248

17) Answer: C
Topic: Parallelism
References: LB16, LH46, SFW10b, SFH16h, WH48b, NCH38a, DK248

18) Answer: C
Topic: Run-On/Fused Sentences and Comma Splice
References: LB36, LH34b&41, SFW11&31&38, SFH35c–d, WH43a, NCH32a–d, DK470

19) Answer: A
Topic: Run-On/Fused Sentences and Comma Splice
References: LB36, LH34b&41, SFW11&31&38, SFH35c–d, WH43a, NCH32a–d, DK470

20) Answer: B
Topic: Fragments
References: LB35, LH40, SFW31a, SFH35a, WH42a, NCH31a–c, DK466

21) Answer: C
Topic: Fragments
References: LB35c, LH40, SFW31a, SFH35a, WH42a, NCH31a–c, DK466

22) Answer: C
Topic: Run-On/Fused Sentences and Comma Splice
References: LB20&36, LH34b&41, SFW11&31&38, SFH35c–d, WH43a, NCH32a–d, DK470

23) Answer: A
Topic: Subject-Verb Agreement
References: LB29d, LH38a–b, SFW33a, SFH22a, WH36b, 39b, NCH29d, DK458

24) Answer: A
Topic: Subject-Verb Agreement
References: LB29j, LH38a–b, SFW33a, SFH22a, WH36b, NCH29d, DK458

25) Answer: C
Topic: Subject-Verb Agreement
References: LB29, LH38a–b, SFW33b, SFH22b, WH36b, NCH2929e–g, DK458

26) Answer: D
Topic: Subject-Verb Agreement
References: LB29, LH38a–b, SFW33c, SFH22a–b, WH36b, NCH29e–g, DK458

27) Answer: C
Topic: Pronoun Case
References: LB30c, LH37d, SFW35c, SFH28a, WH35c, gl, NCH27d, gl–22, DK486

28) Answer: A
Topic: Pronoun Case
References: LB30a, LH37b, SFW35c, SFH28a, WH35b–c, NCH27c, DK486

29) Answer: D
Topic: Pronoun-Antecedent Agreement
References: LB31, LH38c, SFW35b, SFH28a, WH44b, NCH33e, DK473

30) Answer: C
Topic: Pronoun-Antecedent Agreement
References: LB31, LH38c, SFW35c, SFH28a, WH44b, NCH33e, DK473

31) Answer: B
Topic: Pronoun Reference
References: LB32a, LH42, SFW35a, SFH26a, WH44b, NCH33a, DK472

32) Answer: B
Topic: Appropriate Word Usage
References: LB18a, LH48–50, SFW8, SFH15b, WH52c, NCH41a–b, DK253

33) Answer: A
Topic: Appropriate Word Usage
References: LB18b, LH48–50, SFW8, SFH15b, WH52c, NCH41a–b, DK253

34) Answer: B
Topic: Appropriate Word Usage
References: LB18b, LH48–50, SFW8, SFH15b, WH52c, NCH41a–b, DK253

35) Answer: B
Topic: Verb Tense Form
References: LB26d, LH36, SFW34a, SFH23a, WH34a–b, 40a, NCH28a, DK496

36) Answer: C
Topic: Subjunctive
References: LB27a, LH36g, SFW34f, SFH23f, WH34f, NCH28h, DK493

37) Answer: A
Topic: Verb Tense Agreement
References: LB26, LH36&38, SFW34a, SFH23a, WH34b, 40a, NCH28d, DK494

38) Answer: C
Topic: Comparisons
References: LB33c, LH43, SFW32h, SFH28a, WH35b, NCH27f, DK487

39) Answer: B
Topic: Comparisons
References: LB33c, LH43, SFW32h, SFH28a, WH35b, NCH27f, DK487

40) Answer: B
Topic: Comparisons
References: LB33c, LH43, SFW32h, SFH28a, WH35b, NCH27f, DK487

41) Answer: A
Topic: Adjectives and Adverbs
References: LB33a, LH39, SFW9b&32, SFH30c, WH37a, NCH30c, DK498

42) Answer: A
Topic: Adjectives and Adverbs
References: LB33, LH39, SFW9b&32, SFH30c, WH37b, gl, NCH30d, gl–16, DK487

43) Answer: A
Topic: Capitalization
References: LB47, LH57, SFW43b, SFH41b, WH59b, NCH53a–c, DK588

44) Answer: B
Topic: Capitalization
References: LB47, LH57, SFW43b, SFH41b, WH59b, NCH53a–c, DK588

45) Answer: B
Topic: Spelling
References: LB45, LH62, SFW45, SFHgl, WH64a, NCH45a–b, DK586

46) Answer: B
Topic: Spelling
References: LB45, LH62, SFW45, SFHgl, WH64a, NCH45a–b, DK586

47) Answer: B
Topic: Comma Usage
References: LB39a, LH51, SFW38, SFH36a, WH53a, NCH47b, DK528

48) Answer: A
Topic: Quotation Marks
References: LB43a, LH54, SFW40a, SFH38a, WH57a, NCH51a, DK570

49) Answer: D
Topic: Comma Usage, Interrupting Element
References: LB39b, LH51b, SFW38a, SFH35a, WH53d, NCH47e, DK528

50) Answer: B
Topic: Comma Usage, Introductory Element
References: LB39b, LH51b, SFW38a, SFH36a, WH53b, NCH47a, DK528

DIAGNOSTIC TEST H

1) Answer: C
Topic: Wordiness/Redundancies/Conciseness
References: LB20, LH48, SFW8&11, SFH17b–c, WH50a–c, NCH36a–b,h, DK259

2) Answer: D
Topic: Wordiness/Redundancies/Conciseness
References: LB20, LH48, SFW11a, SFH17b–c, WH50a–c, NCH36e, DK259

3) Answer: C
Topic: Wordiness/Wordy Phrases
References: LB20, LH48, SFW11a, SFH17c, WH50a–c, NCH36e, DK259

4) Answer: B
Topic: Denotation/Connotation
References: LB17–19, LH48–50, SFW8d, SFH15b, WH52c, NCH41a–b, DK253

5) Answer: A
Topic: Denotation/Connotation
References: LB17–19, LH48–50, SFW8d, SFH15b, WH52c, NCH41a–b, DK253

6) Answer: C
Topic: Denotation/Connotation
References: LB17–19, LH48–50, SFW8d, SFH15b, WH52c, NCH41a–b, DK253

7) Answer: C
Topic: Dangling Modifiers
References: LB34b, LH34e&43b, SFW32a, SFH30a, WH45b, NCH34e, DK474

8) Answer: C
Topic: Misplaced Modifiers
References: LB34a, LH43a, SFW32a, SFH30a, WH45a, NCH34a, DK474

9) Answer: D
Topic: Misplaced Modifiers
References: LB34a, LH43a, SFW32a, SFH30a, WH45a, NCH34a, DK474

10) Answer: A
Topic: Misplaced Modifiers
References: LB34a, LH43a, SFW32a, SHF30a, WH45a, NCH34a, DK474

11) Answer: A
Topic: Coordination/Subordination
References: LB23, LH47, SFW9e–f, SFH16f, WH49a–c, NCH37a–c, DK246

12) Answer: B
Topic: Coordination/Subordination
References: LB23, LH47, SFW9e–f, SFH16f, WH49a–c, NCH37a–c, DK246

13) Answer: B
Topic: Coordination/Subordination
References: LB23, LH47, SFW9e–f, SFH16f, WH49a–c, NCH37a–c, DK246

14) Answer: A
Topic: Dangling Modifiers
References: LB34b, LH34e&43b, SFW32a, SFH30a, WH45b, NCH34e, DK474

15) Answer: C
Topic: Parallelism
References: LB16c, LH46, SFW10b, SFH16h, WH48b, NCH38a, DK248

16) Answer: C
Topic: Parallelism
References: LB16a, LH46, SFW10b, SFH16h, WH48b, NCH38a, DK248

17) Answer: A
Topic: Parallelism
References: LB16a, LH46, SFW10b, SFH16h, WH48b, NCH38a, DK248

18) Answer: D
Topic: Run-On/Fused Sentences and Comma Splice
References: LB36, LH34b&41, SFW11&31&38, SFH35c–d, WH43a, NCH32a–d, DK470

19) Answer: D
Topic: Run-On/Fused Sentences and Comma Splice
References: LB36, LH34b&41, SFW11&31&38, SFH35c–d, WH43a, NCH32a–d, DK470

20) Answer: B
Topic: Sentence Fragments
References: LB35, LH40, SFW31a, SFH35a, WH42a, NCH31a-–c, DK466

21) Answer: B
Topic: Sentence Fragments
References: LB35, LH40, SFW31a, SFH35a, WH42a, NCH31a–c, DK466

22) Answer: A
Topic: Sentence Fragments
References: LB35, LH40, SFW31a, SFH35a, WH42a, NCH31a–c, DK466

23) Answer: A
Topic: Subject-Verb Agreement
References: LB29, LH38a–b, SFW33c, SFH22b, WH36b, NCH29e, DK456

24) Answer: B
Topic: Subject-Verb Agreement
References: LB29, LH38a–b, SFW33c, SFH22b–c, WH36b, NCH29e–g, DK456

25) Answer: B
Topic: Subject-Verb Agreement
References: LB29, LH38a–b, SFW33a, SFH22a, WH36b, 39b, NCH29d, DK458

26) Answer: A
Topic: Subject-Verb Agreement
References: LB29, LH38a–b, SFW33, SFH22a–b, WH36b, NCH29d,e, DK458

27) Answer: A
Topic: Pronoun Case and Antecedent Agreement
References: LB30a&31d, LH37b&38c, SFW35c, SFH28a–b, WH35b, 39b, NCH27a–c, DK486

28) Answer: C
Topic: Pronoun Case
References: LB30c, LH37d, SFW35c, SFH28a, WH35c, gl, NCH27d, gl–22, DK486

29) Answer: A
Topic: Pronoun Case
References: LB30a, LH37b, SFW35c, SFH28a, WH35b, NCH27c, DK486

30) Answer: A
Topic: Pronoun-Antecedent Agreement
References: LB31c, LH38c, SFW35c, SFH28a, WH33a, 35a, NCH27e, DK486

31) Answer: D
Topic: Pronoun Reference
References: LB32, LH42, SFW35a, SFH26c, WH44b, NCH33a, DK472

32) Answer: B
Topic: Appropriate Word Usage
References: LB18b, LH48–50, SFW8d SFH15b, WH52c, NCH41a–b, DK253

33) Answer: A
Topic: Appropriate Word Usage
References: LB18b, LH48–50, SFW8d, SFH15b, WH52c, NCH41a–b, DK253

34) Answer: B
Topic: Appropriate Word Usage
References: LB18b, LH48–50, SFW8d, SFH15b, WH52c, NCH41a–b, DK253

35) Answer: C
Topic: Verb Tense Form
References: LB26, LH36a–c, SFW34a, SFH23b, WH34a, NCH28b, DK495

36) Answer: A
Topic: Verb Tense Agreement
References: LB27a, LH36, SFW34a, SFH23f, WH34f, NCH28h, DK493

37) Answer: C
Topic: Verb Tense Agreement
References: LB26d, LH36, SFW34a, SFH23a, WH34f, NCH28h, DK494

38) Answer: C
Topic: Comparisons
References: LB16c, LH39c, SFW32h, SFH28a, WH35b, NCH27f, DK487

39) Answer: A
Topic: Comparisons
References: LB16c, LH39c, SFW32h, SFH28a, WH35b, NCH27f, DK487

40) Answer: C
Topic: Comparisons
References: LB16c, LH39c, SFW32h, SFH28a, WH35b, NCH27f, DK487

41) Answer: D
Topic: Adjectives and Adverbs
References: LB33b, LH39, SFW9b&32, SFH30c, WH37a, NCH30a–c, DK487, 498

42) Answer: B
Topic: Adjectives and Adverbs
References: LB33, LH39, SFW9b&32, SFH30c, WH37a, NCH30c, DK487, 498

43) Answer: C
Topic: Capitalization
References: LB47, LH57, SFW43b, SFH41b, WH59b, NCH53a–c, DK588

44) Answer: C
Topic: Capitalization
References: LB47, LH57, SFW43b, SFH41b, WH59b, NCH53a–c, DK588

45Answer: C
Topic: Spelling
References: LB45, LH62, SFW45, SFHgl, WH64a, NCH45a–b, DK586

46) Answer: A
Topic: Spelling
References: LB45, LH62, SFW45, SFHgl, WH64a, NCH45a–b, DK586

47) Answer: B
Topic: Comma and Semicolon usage
References: LB39–41, LH51&52, SFW38&39a, SFH37a–b, WH53e, 54a, NCH48c, 47g, 49a, DK549

48) Answer: B
Topic: Comma Usage
References: LB39a, LH51, SFW38, SFH36, WH53b, NCH47a, DK528

49) Answer: D
Topic: Quotation Marks
References: LB43a, LH54, SFW40a, SFH38a, WH57c, NCH51a, DK570

50) Answer: B
Topic: Semicolon
References: LB40b, LH52a, SFW39a, SFH37a, WH54a, NCH48b, DK549

EXERCISES

EXERCISE A: Sentence Grammar and Structure

Select the letter of the answer that best describes the underlined portion of each sentence.

1) Answer: B
Topic: Adverbs
References: LB33a, LH39, SFW9b&32e–f, SFH30e, WH37a, NCH30c, DK498

2) Answer: A
Topic: Adjectives
References: LB33a, LH39, SFW32b–d, SFH30c, WH37a, NCH30a, DK487

3) Answer: B
Topic: Relative Pronouns
References: LB32, LH37b, SFW35d, SFH26c, WH35a, NCH26a, DK486

4) Answer: C
Topic: Adjectives
References: LB33a, LH39, SFW32b–d, SFH30c, WH37a, NCH30a, DK487

5) Answer: C
Topic: Subject, Sentence Structure
References: LB15a&17b, SFW9, SFH22e, WH33b, NCH26b, DK478

6) Answer: B
Topic: Prepositional Phrase
References: LB21, LH35c, SFW9c, SFH16a, WH33c, NCH26c, DK500

7) Answer: A
Topic: Independent Clause
References: LB21, LH35c, SFW9d SFH16e, WH33c, NCH26c, DK517

8) Answer: C
Topic: Appositive
References: LB39b, LH51b, SFW9d, SFH28a, WH53d, NCH37c, 47e55, DK544

9) Answer: C
Topic: Object
References: LB21, LH35, SFW9, SFH28a, WH33b, NCH26b, DK478

10) Answer: A
Topic: Dependent Clauses
References: LB23, LH35, SFW9d, SFH28a, WH33c, NCH26c, DK469

11) Answer: C
Topic: Conjunctive Adverb
References: LB33, LH39, SFW32e, SFH14a, WH33a, NCH26a, DK505

12) Answer: A
Topic: Subordinating Conjunction
References: LB23, LH35, SFW32e, SFH16d, WH33a, NCH26a, DK522

13) Answer: B
Topic: Infinitive Verb
References: LB25e, LH36, SFW34a, SFH16h, WH33c, NCH26a, DK495

14) Answer: C
Topic: Participle Phrase
References: LB33e, LH35, SFW9c, SFH16c, WH33c, NCH26c, DK469

15) Answer: A
Topic: Proper Noun
References: LB15a, LH57b, SFW9, SFH41b, WH33a, NCH26a, DK480

EXERCISE B: Using Verbs

1) Answer: A
Topic: Irregular Verbs
References: LB25a, LH36d, SFW34c, SFH23b, WH34a, NCH28b, DK494

2) Answer: B
Topic: Helping Verbs
References: LB25d, LH36, SFW34c, SFH23a, WH34b, NCH28c, DK495

3) Answer: A
Topic: Verb Tenses/Irregular
References: LB25a, LH36d, SFW34a, SFH23b, WH34a, NCH28f, DK495

4) Answer: B
Topic: Verb Tenses
References: LB26, LH36, SFW34a, SFH23a, WH34a, NCH28b, DK461

5) Answer: C
Topic: Irregular Verbs/Tenses
References: LB25a, LH36d, SFW34a, SFH23a–b, WH34a, NCH28b, DK494

6) Answer: B
Topic: Irregular Verbs/Tenses
References: LB25a, LH36d, SFW34a, SFH23a–b, WH34a, NCH28b–c, DK495

7) Answer: A
Topic: Verb Tenses
References: LB26b, LH36, SFW34a, SFH23a, WH34b, NCH28b–c, DK461

8) Answer: C
Topic: Verb Tenses
References: LB26, LH36, SFW34a, SFH23a, WH34b, NCH28b–c, DK460

9) Answer: A
Topic: Verb Tenses
References: LB26a, LH36, SFW34a, SFH23a, WH34b, NCH28b–c, DK460

10) Answer: A
Topic: Verb Tenses
References: LB26a, LH36, SFW34a, ASFH23a, WH34b, NCH28b–c, DK460

11) Answer: C
Topic: Verb Tenses
References: LB26, LH36, SFW34a, SFH23a, WH34b, NCH28b–c, DK460

12) Answer: B
Topic: Verb Tenses
References: LB26c, LH36, SFW34a SFH23a, WH34f, NCH28h, DK493

13) Answer: A
Topic: Verb Tenses
References: LB26, LH36, SFW34a, SFH23a, WH34a, NCH28b, DK460

14) Answer: B
Topic: Verb Tenses
References: LB26, LH36, SFW34a, SFH23a, WH34f, NCH28h, DK494

15) Answer: A
Topic: Verb Tenses
References: LB26, LH36, SFW34a, SFH23a, WH34e, NCH28c, DK461

EXERCISE C: Case of Pronouns and Nouns

1) Answer: A
Topic: Pronoun Case
References: LB30a, LH37b, SFW35c, SFH28a, WH35b, NCH27a–c, DK486

2) Answer: B
Topic: Using Who and Whom
References: LB30c, LH37d, SFW35d, SFH28a, WH35c, gl, NCH27d, gl–22, DK486

3) Answer: B
Topic: Personal Pronouns
References: LB30a, LH37b, SFW35, SFH28a, WH35a, NCH27b, DK484

4) Answer: B
Topic: Pronoun Case
References: LB30d, LH37b, SFW35c, SFH28a–c, WH35a, 56b, NCH27a–e, gl–22, DK486

5) Answer: A
Topic: Pronoun Case
References: LB30d, LH37b, SFW35c, SFH28a–c, WH35a, NCH27a–e, DK486

6) Answer: C
Topic: Using Who and Whom
References: LB30c, LH37d, SFW35d, SFH28a, WH35c, gl, NCH27d, gl–22, DK486

7) Answer: B
Topic: Personal Pronouns
References: LB30a, LH37b, SFW35, SFH28a, WH35a, NCH27b–c, DK484

8) Answer: A
Topic: Pronoun Reference
References: LB32, LH42, SFW35a, SFH28a, WH35a, 44b, NCH33b, DK472

9) Answer: B
Topic: Pronouns, Using We and Us
References: LB30, LH37b, SFW35, SFH28a, WH35a, NCH27a, DK473

10) Answer: C
Topic: Reflexive Pronouns
References: LB32, LH37b, SFW35, SFH29d, WH35a, NCH27b, DK486

11) Answer: A
Topic: Using We and Us
References: LB30, LH37b, SFW35, SFH28a, WH35a, NCH27a, DK473

12) Answer: C
Topic: Using Who and Whom
References: LB30c, LH37d, SFW35d, SFH28a, WH35c, NCH27e, DK486

13) Answer: A
Topic: Personal Pronouns
References: LB30b, LH37b, SFW35, SFH28a, WH35a, NCH27a, DK484

14) Answer: C
Topic: Homonyms
References: LB18b, LH49, SFW8d&45, SFHgl, WH56b, gl, NCHgl–22, DKgl

15) Answer: B
Topic: Personal Pronouns
References: LB30a, LH37b, SFW35, SFH28a, WH35b, NCH27b–c, DK484

EXERCISE D: Using Adjectives and Adverbs

Select the letter of the correct answer.

1) Answer: B
Topic: Adjective or Adverb?
References: LB33a, LH39b, SFW32, SFH30, WH37a, NCH30c, DK487, 498

2) Answer: B
Topic: Using Good/Well and Bad/Badly
References: LB33b, LH39b, SFW32e, SFH30c, WH37b, gl, NCH30d, gl–16, DK498

3) Answer: B
Topic: Adjective or Adverb?
References: LB33a, LH39b, SFW32 SFH30, WH37a–b, NCH30c, 487, 498, DK487, 498

4) Answer: C
Topic: Comparative/Superlative Forms
References: LB33c, LH39c, SFW32h, SFH30h, WH37c, NCH30e, DK487

5) Answer: C
Topic: Adjective or Adverb?
References: LB33a, LH39b, SFW32, SFH30, WH37a, NCH30c, DK487, 498

6) Answer: B
Topic: Using Good/Well and Bad/Badly
References: LB33b, LH39, SFW32e, SFH30c, WH37b, gl, NCH30dm gl–16, DK498

7) Answer: C
Topic: Adjective or Adverb?
References: LB33a, LH39b, SFW32, SFH30

8) Answer: A
Topic: Adjectives and Adverbs
References: LB33a, LH39, SFW32b–c, SF30b-e, WH62b, NCH30, DK487

9) Answer: B
Topic: Adjectives and Adverbs
References: LB33, LH39, SFW32, SFH30, WH37a, NCH30c, DK487, 498

10) Answer: A
Topic: Adjectives and Adverbs
References: LB33, LH39, SFW32, SFH30, WH37a, NCH30a, DK487, 498

11) Answer: B
Topic: Adjectives and Adverbs
References: LB33, LH39, SFW32, SFH30, WH37a, NCH30a, DK487, 498

12) Answer: A
Topic: Adjectives and Adverbs
References: LB33, LH39, SFW32, SFH30, WH37a, NCH30c, DK487, 498

13) Answer: B
Topic: Adjectives and Adverbs
References: LB33, LH39, SFW32, SFH30, WH37a, NCH30c, DK487, 498

14) Answer: A
Topic: Adjective or Adverb?
References: LB33a, LH39b, SFW32, SFH30, WH37a, NCH30c, DK487, 498

15) Answer: C
Topic: Adjectives and Adverbs
References: LB33, LH39, SFW32, SFH30, WH37a, NCH30c, DK487, 498

EXERCISE E: Revising for Subject-Verb Agreement

1) Answer: A
Topic: Verb Agreement with Indefinite Pronoun Subject
References: LB29e, LH38, SFW33b, SFH22b, WH36b, NCH29e, DK459

2) Answer: B
Topic: Maintaining Agreement
References: LB29b, LH38, SFW33, SFH22a, WH36b, NCH29e, DK459

3) Answer: A
Topic: Maintaining Agreement
References: LB29b, LH38, SFW33, SFH22a, WH36b, NCH29a, DK459

4) Answer: A
Topic: Separated Subject, Verb Agreement
References: LB29b, LH38, SFW33, SFH22d, WH36b, 39c, NCH29e, DK459

5) Answer: B
Topic: Agreement in Inverted Sentences
References: LB29, LH38, SFW33, SFH22d, WH36b, NCH29i, DK456

6) Answer: A
Topic: Separated Subject
References: LB29b, LH38, SFW33, SFH22d, WH36b, 39b, NCH29e, DK456

7) Answer: B
Topic: Separated Subject
References: LB29b, LH38, SFW33, SFH22d, WH36b, 39b, NCH29b, DK456

8) Answer: B
Topic: Separated Subject
References: LB29b, LH38, SFW33, SFH22d, WH36b, 39b, NCH29b, DK456

9) Answer: B
Topic: Compound Subject
References: LB19a, LH38, SFW33, SFH22e, WH36b, 39b, NCH29d, DK458

10) Answer: B
Topic: Separated Subject
References: LB29b, LH38, SFW33, SFH22d, WH36b, 39b, NCH29b, DK456

11) Answer: B
Topic: Relative Pronoun Subjects, Collective Nouns
References: LB29a, LH38, SFW33d, SFH22c, WH36b, NCH29f, DK459

12) Answer: A
Topic: Relative Pronoun Subjects, Collective Nouns
References: LB29a, LH38, SFW33d, SFH22c, WH36b, NCH29b, DK459

13) Answer: B
Topic: Separated Subject
References: LB29b, LH38, SFW33d, SFH22d, WH36b, 39b, NCH29e, DK456

14) Answer: B
Topic: Relative Pronoun Subject
References: LB29, LH38, SFW33d, SFH22e, WH36b, 39b, NCH29d, DK458

EXERCISE F: Revising for Sentence Fragments

1) Answer: B
Topic: Clear and Effective Sentences, Phrase Fragments
References: LB19&20, LH45&46, SFW10&11&31, SFH30a, WH42a&50c, NCH31a–c, DK226

2) Answer: C
Topic: Clear and Effective Sentences, Phrase Fragments
References: LB19&20, LH45&46, SFW10&11&31, SFH30a, WH42a&50c, NCH31a–c, DK266

197

3) Answer: A
Topic: Clear and Effective Sentences, Phrase Fragments
References: LB19&20, LH45&46, SFW10&11&31, SFH30a, WH42a, 50c, NCH31a–c, DK266

4) Answer: B
Topic: Dependent Clauses
References: LB22, LH35c, SFW9d, SFH30a, WH33c, NCH26c, DK469

5) Answer: C
Topic: Sentence Fragments
References: LB35, LH40, SFW31, SFH35a, WH42a, NCH31a–c, DK466

6) Answer: C
Topic: Sentence Fragments
References: LB35, LH40, SFW31, SFH35a, WH42a, NCH31a–c, DK466

7) Answer: B
Topic: Sentence Fragments
References: LB35, LH40, SFW31, SFH35a, WH42a, NCH31a–c, DK466

8) Answer: A
Topic: Sentence Fragments
References: LB35, LH40, SFW31, SFH35a, WH42a, NCH31a–c, DK466

9) Answer: B
Topic: Sentence Fragments
References: LB35, LH40, SFW31, SFH35a, WH42a, NCH31a–c, DK466

10) Answer: C
Topic: Sentence Fragments
References: LB35, LH40, SFW31, SFH35a, WH42a, NCH31a–c, DK466

11) Answer: C
Topic: Sentence Fragments
References: LB35, LH40, SFW31, SFH35a, WH42a, NCH31a–c, DK466

12) Answer: A
Topic: Sentence Fragments
References: LB35, LH40, SFW31, SFH35a, WH42a, NCH31a–c, DK466

EXERCISE G: Comma Splices and Fused Sentences

1) Answer: B
Topic: Semicolon
References: LB40a, LH52a, SFW39a, SFH37a, WH54a, NHC48a, DK549

2) Answer: C
Topic: Comma and Coordinating Conjunctions
References: LB39a, LH51i, SFW38, SFH36c, WH53a, NHC47b, DK247

3) Answer: A
Topic: Semicolon and Conjunctive Adverb
References: LB40b, LH52a, SFW32f&39a, SFH37a, WH54a, NCH48b, DK505, 549

4) Answer: B
Topic: Semicolon and Conjunctive Adverb
References: LB40b, LH52a, SFW32f&39a, SFH37a, WH54a, NCH48b, DK505, 549

5) Answer: C
Topic: Semicolon
References: LB40a, LH52a, SFW39a, SFH37a, WH54a, NCH48a, DK549

6) Answer: A
Topic: Semicolon
References: LB40a, LH52a, SFW39a, SFH37a, WH54a, NCH48a, DK549

7) Answer: B
Topic: Semicolon
References: LB40a, LH52a, SFW39a, SFH37a, WH54a, NCH48a, DK549

8) Answer: A
Topic: Comma and Coordinating Conjunctions
References: LB39a, LH51, SFW38, SFH36c, WH53a, NCH47b, DK247

9) Answer: B
Topic: Comma Splice
References: LB36a, LH41, SFW38, SHF35c, WH43a, NCH32a–d, DK470

10) Answer: B
Topic: Colon
References: LB41, LH52b, SFW39b, SFH37b, WH54b, NCH49a, DK554

11) Answer: A
Topic: Comma Splice
References: LB36a, LH41, SFW38, SHF35c, WH43a, NCH32a–d, DK470

12) Answer: B
Topic: Colon
References: LB41, LH52b, SFW39b, SFH37b, WH54b, NCH49a, DK554

13) Answer: A
Topic: Comma Splice
References: LB36a, LH41, SFW38, SFH35c, WH43a, NCH32a–d, DK470

14) Answer: B
Topic: Semicolon
References: LB40, LH52a, SFW39a, SFH37a, WH54a, NCH48a, DK549

15) Answer: C
Topic: Comma Splice
References: LB36b, LH41, SFW38, SFH35c, WH43a, NCH32a–d, DK470

EXERCISE H: Revising Misplaced and Dangling Modifiers

1) Answer: B
Topic: Misplaced Modifiers
References: LB34a, LH43a, SFW32a, SFH30a, WH45a, NCH34a, DK474

2) Answer: A
Topic: Misplaced Modifiers
References: LB34a, LH43a, SFW32a, SFH30a, WH45a, NCH34a, DK474

3) Answer: B
Topic: Misplaced Modifiers
References: LB34a, LH43a, SFW32a, SFH30a, WH45a, NCH34a, DK474

4) Answer: A
Topic: Misplaced Modifiers
References: LB34a, LH43a, SFW32a, SFH30a, WH45a, NCH34a, DK474

5) Answer: B
Topic: Misplaced Modifiers
References: LB34a, LH43a, SFW32a, SFH30a, WH45a, NCH34a, DK474

6) Answer: B
Topic: Misplaced Modifiers
References: LB34a, LH43a, SFW32a, SFH30a, WH45a, NCH34a, DK474

7) Answer: B
Topic: Misplaced Modifiers
References: LB34a, LH43a, SFW32a, SFH30a, WH45a, NCH34a, DK474

8) Answer: A
Topic: Interrupting Modifiers
References: LB34b, LH43c, SFW32, SFH30a, WH45c, NCH34d, DK474

9) Answer: B
Topic: Dangling Modifiers
References: LB34b, LH34e&43b, SFW32a, SFH30a, WH45b, NCH34e, DK474

10) Answer: B
Topic: Misplaced Modifiers
References: LB34a, LH43a, SFW32a, SFH30a, WH45a, NCH34a, DK474

11) Answer: B
Topic: Misplaced Modifiers
References: LB34a, LH43a, SFW32a, SFH30a, WH45a, NCH34a, DK474

12) Answer: B
Topic: Dangling Modifiers
References: LB34b, LH34e&43b, SFW32a, SFH30a, WH45b, NCH34e, DK474

13) Answer: A
Topic: Interrupting Modifiers
References: LB34b, LH43c, SFW32&38, SFH30a, WH44c, NCH34d, DK474

14) Answer: B
Topic: Misplaced Modifiers
References: LB34a, LH43a, SFW32a, SFH30a, WH45a, NCH34a, DK474

15) Answer: A
Topic: Misplaced Modifiers
References: LB34a, LH43a, SFW32a, SFH30a, WH45a, NCH34a, DK474

EXERCISE I: Revising for Shifts and Mixed Construction

1) Answer: B
Topic: Shifts and Mixed Construction
References: LB15&17, LH45a, SFW9&10, SFH23, WH46a, NCH35a, DK236

2) Answer: C
Topic: Shifts and Mixed Construction
References: LB15&17, LH45a, SFW9&10, SFH23, WH46a, NCH35a, DK236

3) Answer: A
Topic: Shifts and Mixed Construction
References: LB15&17, LH45a, SFW9&10, SFH23, WH46b, NCH35b, DK236

4) Answer: C
Topic: Shifts and Mixed Construction
References: LB15&17, LH45a, SFW9&10, SFH23, WH46a, NCH35a, DK236

5) Answer: A
Topic: Shifts and Mixed Construction
References: LB15&17, LH45a, SFW9&10, SFH23, WH46a, NCH35a, DK236

6) Answer: B
Topic: Shifts and Mixed Construction
References: LB15&17, LH45a, SFW9&10, SFH23, WH46b, NCH35b, DK236

7) Answer: B
Topic: Shifts and Mixed Construction
References: LB15&17, LH45a, SFW9&10, SFH23, WH46a, NCH35b, DK236

8) Answer: C
Topic: Shifts and Mixed Construction
References: LB15&17, LH45a, SFW9&10, SFH23, WH46a, NCH35a, DK236

9) Answer: B
Topic: Shifts and Mixed Construction
References: LB15&17, LH45a, SFW9&10, SFH23, WH46a, NCH35b, DK236

10) Answer: C
Topic: Shifts and Mixed Construction
References: LB15&17, LH45a, SFW9&10, SFH23, WH46a, NCH35a, DK236

11) Answer: C
Topic: Shifts and Mixed Construction
References: LB15&17, LH45a, SFW9&10, SFH23, WH46a, NCH35a, DK236

12) Answer: B
Topic: Shifts and Mixed Construction
References: LB15&17, LH45a, SFW9&10, SFH23, WH46a, NCH35a, DK236

13) Answer: A
Topic: Shifts and Mixed Construction
References: LB15&17, LH45a, SFW9&10, SFH23, WH46a, NCH34a, DK236

14) Answer: B
Topic: Shifts and Mixed Construction
References: LB15&17, LH45a, SFW9&10, SFH23, WH46a, NCH35a, DK236

15) Answer: B
Topic: Shifts and Mixed Construction
References: LB15&17, LH45a, SFW9&10, SFH23, WH46a, NCH35a, DK236

EXERCISE J: Revising for Pronoun *References* and Antecedent Agreement

1) Answer: A
Topic: Pronoun Reference and Antecedent Agreement
References: LB31, LH38c&42, SFW35a–b, SFH22b, WH44b, NCH33e, DK473

2) Answer: B
Topic: Pronoun Reference and Antecedent Agreement
References: LB31, LH38c&42, SFW35a–b, SFH22b, WH44b, NCH33e, DK473

3) Answer: B
Topic: Pronoun Reference and Antecedent Agreement
References: LB31, LH38c&42, SFW35a–b, SFH22b, WH44b, NCH33e, DK473

4) Answer: C
Topic: Pronoun Reference and Antecedent Agreement
References: LB31, LH3, SFH22b 8c&42, SFW35a–b, SFH22b, WH44b, NCH33e, DK473

5) Answer: C
Topic: Pronoun Reference and Antecedent Agreement
References: LB31, LH38c&42, SFW35a–b, SFH22b, WH44b, NCH33e, DK473

6) Answer: A
Topic: Pronoun Reference and Antecedent Agreement
References: LB31, LH38c&42, SFW35a–b, SFH22b, WH44b, NCH33b, DK473

7) Answer: C
Topic: Pronoun Reference and Antecedent Agreement
References: LB31, LH38c&42, SFW35a–b, SFH22b, WH44b, NCH33a, DK473

8) Answer: B
Topic: Pronoun Reference and Antecedent Agreement
References: LB31, LH38c&42, SFW35a–b, SFH22b, WH44b, NCH33b, DK473

9) Answer: B
Topic: Pronoun Reference and Antecedent Agreement
References: LB31, LH38c&42, SFW35a–b, SFH22b, WH44b, NCH33b, DK473

10) Answer: A
Topic: Pronoun Reference and Antecedent Agreement
References: LB31, LH38c&42, SFW35a–b, SFH22b, WH44b, NCH33a, DK473

11) Answer: B
Topic: Pronoun Reference and Antecedent Agreement
References: LB31, LH38c&42, SFW35a–b, SFH22b, WH44b, NCH33b, DK473

12) Answer: C
Topic: Pronoun Reference and Antecedent Agreement
References: LB31, LH38c&42, SFW35a–b, SFH22b, WH44b, NCH33a, DK473

13) Answer: B
Topic: Pronoun Reference and Antecedent Agreement
References: LB31, LH38c&42, SFW35a–b, SFH22b, WH44b, NCH33b, DK473

14) Answer: C
Topic: Pronoun Reference and Antecedent Agreement
References: LB31, LH38c&42, SFH22b, SFW35a–b, WH44b, NCH33a, DK473

15) Answer: B
Topic: Pronoun Reference and Antecedent Agreement
References: LB31, LH38c&42, SFW35a–b, SFH22b, WH44b, NCH33b, DK473

EXERCISE K: Mixed or Incomplete Sentences

1) Answer: B
Topic: Mixed or Incomplete Construction
References: LB15&20, LH45, SFW10&11, SFH23, WH47a, NCH35a, DK466

2) Answer: A
Topic: Mixed or Incomplete Construction
References: LB15&20, LH45, SFW10&11, SFH23, WH47a, NCH35d, DK466

3) Answer: B
Topic: Mixed or Incomplete Construction
References: LB15&20, LH45, SFW10&11, SFH23, WH47a, NCH35a, DK466

4) Answer: B
Topic: Mixed or Incomplete Construction
References: LB15&20, LH45, SFW10&11, SFH23, WH47a, NCH35d, DK466

5) Answer: A
Topic: Mixed or Incomplete Construction
References: LB15&20, LH45, SFW10&11, SFH23, WH47a, NCH35d, DK466

6) Answer: B
Topic: Mixed or Incomplete Construction
References: LB15&20, LH45, SFW10&11, SFH23, WH47a, NCH35d, DK466

7) Answer: A
Topic: Mixed or Incomplete Construction
References: LB15&20, LH45, SFW10&11, SFH23, WH47a, NCH35d, DK466

8) Answer: B
Topic: Mixed or Incomplete Construction
References: LB15&20, LH45, SFW10&11, SFH23, WH47a, NCH35d, DK466

9) Answer: B
Topic: Mixed or Incomplete Construction
References: LB15&20, LH45, SFW10&11, SFH23, WH47a, NCH35d, DK466

10) Answer: A
Topic: Mixed or Incomplete Construction
References: LB15&20, LH45, SFW10&11, SFH23, WH47a, NCH35d, DK466

11) Answer: B
Topic: Mixed or Incomplete Construction
References: LB15&20, LH45, SFW10&11, SFH23, WH47a, NCH35d, DK466

12) Answer: A
Topic: Mixed or Incomplete Construction
References: LB15&20, LH45, SFW10&11, SFH23, WH47a, NCH35d, DK466

13) Answer: B
Topic: Mixed or Incomplete Construction
References: LB15&20, LH45, SFW10&11, SFH23, WH47a, NCH35d, DK466

14) Answer: B
Topic: Mixed or Incomplete Construction
References: LB15&20, LH45, SFW10&11, SFH23, WH47a, NCH5d, DK466

15) Answer: B
Topic: Mixed or Incomplete Construction
References: LB15&20, LH45, SFW10&11, SFH23, WH47a, NCH35d, DK466

EXERCISE L: Revising for Coordination, Subordination, and Emphasis

1) Answer: C
Topic: Coordination, Emphasis
References: LB15c, LH47, SFW9e, SFH16f, WH49a–c, NCH37a–c, DK246

2) Answer: C
Topic: Coordination, Emphasis
References: LB15c, LH47, SFW9e, SFH16f, WH49a–c, NCH37a–c, DK246

3) Answer: C
Topic: Coordination
References: LB15c, LH47a–b, SFW9e, SFH16f, WH49a–c, NCH37a–c, DK246

4) Answer: A
Topic: Subordination
References: LB15d, LH47c–d, SFW9f, SFH16g, WH49a–c, NCH37a–c, DK246

5) Answer: C
Topic: Coordination
References: LB15c, LH47a–b, SFW9e, SFH16f, WH49a–c, NCH37a–c, DK246

6) Answer: C
Topic: Coordination, Emphasis
References: LB15c, LH47, SFW9e, SFH16f, WH49a–c, NCH37a–c, DK246

7) Answer: A
Topic: Subordination
References: LB15d, LH47c–d, SFW9f, SFH16g, WH49a–c, NCH37a–c, DK246

8) Answer: A
Topic: Coordination
References: LB15c, LH47a–b, SFW9e, SFH16f, WH49a–c, NCH37a–c, DK246

9) Answer: A
Topic: Coordination
References: LB15c, LH47a–b, SFW9e, SFH16f, WH49a–c, NCH37a–c, DK246

10) Answer: B
Topic: Coordination/Subordination
References: LB15c–d, LH47, SFW9e–f, SFH16f–g, WH49a–c, NCH37a–c, DK246

EXERCISE M: Writing and Revising to Achieve Parallelism

1) Answer: B
Topic: Series, Lists - Parallelism
References: LB16d, LH46c, SFW10b, SFH16h, WH48b–c NCH38a, DK248

2) Answer: A
Topic: Series, Lists - Parallelism
References: LB16d, LH46c, SFW10b, SFH16h, WH48b–c, NCH38a, DK248

3) Answer: C.
Topic: Pairs, Coherence - Parallelism
References: LB16a, LH46, SFW10b, SFH16h, WH48b, NCH38a, DK248

4) Answer: A
Topic: Series, Lists - Parallelism
References: LB16d, LH46c, SFW10b, SFH16h, WH48b–c, NCH38a, DK248

5) Answer: C
Topic: Pairs, Coherence - Parallelism
References: LB16a, LH46, SFW10b, SFH16h, WH48b, NCH38a, DK248

6) Answer: C
Topic: Series, Lists - Parallelism
References: LB16d, LH46c, SFW10b, SFH16h, WH48b–c, NCH38a, DK248

7) Answer: B
Topic: Series, Lists - Parallelism
References: LB16d, LH46c, SFW10b, SFH16h, WH48b–c, NCH38a, DK248

8) Answer: B
Topic: Pairs, Coherence - Parallelism
References: LB16d, LH46, SFW10b, SFH16h, WH48b, NCH38e, DK248

9) Answer: A
Topic: Series, Lists - Parallelism
References: LB16d, LH46c, SFW10b, SFH16h, WH48b–c, NCH38a, DK248

10) Answer: C
Topic: Pairs, Coherence - Parallelism
References: LB16a, LH46, SFW10b, SFH16h, WH48b, NCH38a–e, DK248

11) Answer: B
Topic: Series, Lists - Parallelism
References: LB16d, LH46c, SFW10b, SFH16h, WH48b–c, NCH38a, DK248

12) Answer: A
Topic: Pairs, Coherence - Parallelism
References: LB16a, LH46, SFW10b, SFH16h, WH48b, NCH38a–e, DK248

13) Answer: C
Topic: Series, Lists - Parallelism
References: LB16d, LH46c, SFW10b, SFH16h, WH48b–c, NCH38a , DK248

14) Answer: A
Topic: Series, Lists - Parallelism
References: LB16d, LH46c, SFW10b, SFH16h, WH48b–c, NCH38a, DK248

EXERCISE N: Diction, Choosing the Right Word

1) Answer: B
Topic: Slang
References: LB18a&20g, LH50, SFW8d, SFW15b, WH52c, NCH41a–b, DK253

2) Answer: A
Topic: Denotation/Connotation
References: LB17–19, LH49, SFW8d, SFH15b, WH52c, NCH41a–b, DK253

3) Answer: C
Topic: Denotation/Connotation
References: LB17–19, LH49, SFW8d, SFH15b, WH52c, NCH41a–b, DK253

4) Answer: A
Topic: Denotation/Connotation
References: LB17–19, LH49, SFW8d, SFH15b, WH52c, NCH41a–b, DK253

5) Answer: C
Topic: Denotation/Connotation
References: LB17–19, LH49, SFW8d, SFH15b, WH52c, NCH41a–b, DK253

6) Answer: C
Topic: Denotation/Connotation
References: LB17–19, LH49, SFW8d, SFH15b, WH52c, NCH41a–b, DK253

7) Answer: A
Topic: Denotation/Connotation
References: LB17–19, LH49, SFW8d, SFH15b, WH52c, NCH41a–b, DK253

8) Answer: B
Topic: Denotation/Connotation
References: LB17–19, LH49, SFW8d, SFH15b, WH52c, NCH41a–b, DK253

9) Answer: A
Topic: Denotation/Connotation
References: LB17–19, LH49, SFW8d, SFH15b, WH52c, NCH41a–b, DK253

10) Answer: A
Topic: Slang
References: LB18a&20g, LH50, SFW8, SFH15b, WH52c, NCH41d, DK253

11) Answer: B
Topic: Denotation/Connotation
References: LB17–19, LH49, SFW8d, SFH15b, WH52c, NCH41a–b, DK253

12) Answer: B
Topic: Denotation/Connotation *References*: LB17–19, LH49, SFW8d, SFH15b, WH52c, NCH41a–b, DK253

13) Answer: A
Topic: Denotation/Connotation
References: LB17–19, LH49, SFW8d, SFH15b, WH52c, NCH41a–b, DK253

14) Answer: A
Topic: Denotation/Connotation
References: LB17–19, LH49, SFW8d, SFH15b, WH52c, NCH41a–b, DK253

15) Answer: C
Topic: Denotation/Connotation
References: LB17–19, LH49, SFW8d, SFH15b, WH52c, NCH41a–b, DK253

EXERCISE O: Learning the Conventions of Spelling

1) Answer: B
Topic: Homonyms
References: LB18&45, LH49, SFW8d&45, SFHgl, WHgl, NCH45b&gl–15, DKgl

2) Answer: C
Topic: Spelling
References: LB45, LH62, SFW45, SFHgl, WH64a, NCH45b, DK586

3) Answer: A
Topic: Spelling
References: LB45, LH62, SFW45, SFHgl, WH64a, NCH45a, DK586

4) Answer: A
Topic: Spelling
References: LB45, LH62, SFW45, SFHgl, WH64a, NCHa, DK586

5) Answer: C
Topic: Spelling
References: LB45, LH62, SFW45, SFHgl, WH64a, NCHa–d, DK586

6) Answer: B
Topic: Spelling
References: LB45, LH62, SFW45, SFHgl, WH64a, NCHa–d, DK586

7) Answer: A
Topic: Spelling
References: LB45, LH62, SFW45, SFHgl, WH64a, NCHa–d, DK586

8) Answer: A
Topic: Spelling
References: LB45, LH62, SFW45, SFHgl, WH64a, NCH45a–d, DK586

9) Answer: A
Topic: Spelling
References: LB45, LH62, SFW45, SFHgl, WH64a, NCH45a–d, DK586

10) Answer: B
Topic: Spelling
References: LB45, LH62, SFW45, SFHgl, WH64a, NCH45a–d, DK586

11) Answer: A
Topic: Distinguishing Between ie and ei
References: LB45, LH62, SFW45, SFHgl, WH64a, NCH45d, DK586

12) Answer: C
Topic: Spelling
References: LB45, LH62, SFW45, SFHgl, WH64a, NCH45a–d, DK586

13) Answer: C
Topic: Spelling
References: LB45, LH62, SFW45, SFHgl, WH64a, NCH45a–d, DK586

14) Answer: C
Topic: Distinguishing Between ie and ei
References: LB45, LH62, SFW45, SFHgl, WH64a, NCH45d, DK586

15) Answer: B
Topic: Spelling
References: LB45, LH62, SFW45, SFHgl, WH64a, NCH45a–d, DK586

EXERCISE P: Using End Punctuation

1) Answer: B
Topic: Quotation Marks, Exclamation Points
References: LB38c, LH54&55c, SFW37c&40a, SFH34c, WH55c&57a, NCH46g&51e, DK570&583

2) Answer: C
Topic: Periods
References: LB38a, LH55a, SFW37a, SFH34a, WH55b, NCH46e, DK582

3) Answer: C
Topic: Periods
References: LB38a, LH55a, SFW37a, SFH34a, WH55a, NCH46a, DK580

4) Answer: A
Topic: Question Marks
References: LB38b, LH55b, SFW37b, SFH34b, WH55b, NCH46e&51e, DK582

5) Answer: B
Topic: Periods
References: LB38a, LH55a, SFW37a, SFH34a, WH55a, NCH46a&51e, DK580

6) Answer: B
Topic: Question Marks
References: LB38b, LH55b, SFW37b, SFH34b, WH55b, NCH46e&51e, DK582

7) Answer: A
Topic: Exclamation Points
References: LB38c, LH55c, SFW37c, SFH34c, WH55c, NCH46g, DK583

8) Answer: C
Topic: Periods
References: LB38a, LH55a, SFW37a, SFH34a, WH55a, NCH46a, DK580

9) Answer: A
Topic: Periods
References: LB38a, LH55a, SFW37a, SFH34a, WH55a, NCH46a, DK580

10) Answer: C
Topic: Periods
References: LB38a, LH55a, SFW37a, SFH34a, WH55a, NCH46a, DK580

11) Answer: C
Topic: Question Marks
References: LB38b, LH55b, SFW37b, SFH34b, WH55b, NCH46e, DK582

12) Answer: A
Topic: Periods
References: LB38a, LH55a, SFW37a, SFH34a, WH55a, NCH46a, DK580

13) Answer: C
Topic: Periods
References: LB38a, LH55a, SFW37a, SFH34a, WH55a, NCH46a, DK581

14) Answer: B
Topic: Periods
References: LB38a, LH55a, SFW37a, SFH34a, WH55a, NCH46a&51e, DK580

15) Answer: A
Topic: Periods
References: LB38a, LH55a, SFW37a, SFH34a, WH55a, NCH46a, DK580

EXERCISE Q: Using Commas

1) Answer: A
Topic: Commas, Misuse
References: LB39h, LH51j, SFW38d, SFH36d, WH53a–h, NCH47j, DK528

2) Answer: C
Topic: Commas, Nonessential Phrases
References: LB39h, LH51c, SFW38, SFH28a, WH53d, NCH47e, DK528

3) Answer: B
Topic: Commas
References: LB39, LH51, SFW38, SFH36a, WH53c, NCH47e, DK528

4) Answer: C
Topic: Commas in a Series
References: LB39d, LH51e, SFW38a, SFH36a, WH53e, NCH47c, DK528

5) Answer: C
Topic: Commas, Interrupting Phrases
References: LB39b, LH51b, SFW38a, SFH36b, WH53a, NCH47e, DK528

6) Answer: C
Topic: Commas, Misuse
References: LB39h, LH51j, SFW38d, SFH36d, WH53a–h, NCH47j, DK528

7) Answer: B
Topic: Commas, Interrupting Phrases
References: LB39b, LH51b, SFW38a, SFH36b, WH53d, NCH47e, DK528

8) Answer: A
Topic: Commas
References: LB39a, LH51, SFW38, SFH36a, WH53a–h, NCH47b, DK528

9) Answer: A
Topic: Comma Usage
References: LB39, LH51, SFW38SFH36a, WH53c, NCH47a, DK528

10) Answer: A
Topic: Commas
References: LB39a, LH51, SFW38, SFH36a, WH53a, NCH47b, DK528

11) Answer: A
Topic: Commas
References: LB39, LH51, SFW38, SFH36a, WH53b, NCH47a, DK528

12) Answer: B
Topic: Commas
References: LB39, LH51, SFW38, SFH36d, WH53d, NCH47e, DK528

EXERCISE R: Using the Semicolon

1) Answer: A
Topic: Semicolon with Conjunctive Adverbs
References: LB40b, LH51a, SFW32&39a, SFH37a, WH54a, NCH48b, DK505, 549

2) Answer: C
Topic: Semicolon with Independent Clauses
References: LB40a, LH51a, SFW39a, SFH37a, WH54a, NCH48a, DK549

3) Answer: B
Topic: Semicolon with Independent Clauses
References: LB40a, LH51a, SFW39a, SFH37a, WH54a, NCH48b, DK549

4) Answer: C
Topic: Semicolon with Independent Clauses
References: LB40a, LH51a, SFW39a, SFH37a, WH54a, NCH48b, DK549

5) Answer: A
Topic: Semicolon with Independent Clauses
References: LB40a, LH51a, SFW39a, SFH37a, WH54a, NCH48b, DK549

6) Answer: B
Topic: Semicolon
References: LB40, LH51a, SFW39a, SFH37a, WH54a, NCH48e, DK549

7) Answer: A
Topic: Semicolon with Independent Clauses
References: LB40a, LH51a, SFW39a, SFH37a, WH54a, NCH48b, DK549

8) Answer: A
Topic: Semicolon with Independent Clauses
References: LB40a, LH51a, SFW39a, SFH37a, WH54a, NCH48b, DK549

9) Answer: B
Topic: Semicolon with Independent Clauses
References: LB40a, LH51a, SFW39a, SFH37a, WH54a, NCH48b, DK549

10) Answer: B
Topic: Semicolon with Independent Clauses
References: LB40a, LH51a, SFW39a, SFH37a, WH54a, NCH48b, DK549

11) Answer: C
Topic: Semicolon with Independent Clauses
References: LB40a, LH51a, SFW39a, SFH37a, WH54a, NCH48b, DK549

12) Answer: B
Topic: Semicolon
References: LB40c, LH51a, SFW39a, SFH37a, WH54a, NCH48b, DK549

13) Answer: C
Topic: Semicolon, Misuse
References: LB40d, LH51a, SFW39a, SFH37a, WH54a, NCH48b, DK549

EXERCISE S: Using Apostrophes

1) Answer: A
Topic: Apostrophes, Possession
References: LB42a, LH53a, SFW44a, SFH25a, WH56a, NCH5050a, DK483

2) Answer: B
Topic: Apostrophes, Possession
References: LB42a, LH53a, SFW44a, SFH28c, WH56a, NCH50a, DK483

214

3) Answer: A
Topic: Apostrophes, Contractions
References: LB42, LH53b, SFW44a, SFH28c, WH56b, NCH50b, DK569

4) Answer: A
Topic: Apostrophes, Possession
References: LB42a, LH53a, SFW44a, SFH25a, WH56a, NCH50a, DK483

5) Answer: C
Topic: Apostrophes, Possession
References: LB42a, LH53a, SFW44a, SFH25a, WH56a, NCH50a, DK483

6) Answer: B
Topic: Apostrophes, Contractions
References: LB42, LH53b, SFW44a, SFH28c, WH56b, NCH50b, DK569

7) Answer: A
Topic: Apostrophes, Contractions
References: LB42, LH53b, SFW44a, SFH28c, WH56b, NCH50b, DK569

8) Answer: C
Topic: Apostrophes, Plurals
References: LB42d, LH53a, SFW44a, SFH25b, WH56a, NCH50c, DK483

9) Answer: B
Topic: Apostrophes, Contractions
References: LB42, LH53b, SFW44a, SFH28c, WH56b, NCH50b, DK569

10) Answer: A
Topic: Apostrophes, Possession
References: LB42a, LH53a, SFW44a, SFH25b, WH56a, NCH50c, DK483

11) Answer: B
Topic: Apostrophes, Contractions
References: LB42c, LH53b, SFW44a, SFH28c, WH56b, NCH50b, DK569

12) Answer: B
Topic: Apostrophes, Possession
References: LB42a, LH53a, SFW44a, SFH25a, WH56a, NCH50a, DK483

13) Answer: A
Topic: Apostrophes, Possession
References: LB42a, LH53a, SFW44a, SFH25b, WH56a, NCH50a, DK483

14) Answer: A
Topic: Apostrophes, Contractions
References: LB42, LH53b, SFW44a, SFH28c, WH56b, NCH50d, DK569

15) Answer: B
Topic: Apostrophes, Contractions
References: LB42, LH53b, SFW44a, SFH28c, WH56b, NCH50b, DK569

EXERCISE T: Using Quotation Marks

1) Answer: B
Topic: Direct Quotes
References: LB43a, LH54, SFW40a, SFH38a, WH57a, NCH51a, DK570

2) Answer: C
Topic: Direct Quotes
References: LB43a, LH54, SFW40a, SFH38a, WH57a, NCH51a, DK570

3) Answer: B
Topic: Direct Quotes
References: LB43a, LH54, SFW40a, SFH38a, WH57a, NCH51a, DK570

4) Answer: C
Topic: Direct Quotes
References: LB43a, LH54, SFW40a, SFH38a, WH57d, NCH51d, DK570

5) Answer: A
Topic: Direct Quotes
References: LB43a, LH54, SFW40a, SFH38a, WH57c, NCH51c, DK570

6) Answer: C
Topic: Direct Quotes
References: LB43a, LH54, SFW40a, SFH38a, WH57a, NCH51a, DK570

7) Answer: C
Topic: Direct Quotes
References: LB43a, LH54, SFW40a, SFH38a, WH57c, NCH51a, DK570

8) Answer: B
Topic: Direct Quotes
References: LB43a, LH54, SFW40a, SFH38a, WH57a, NCH51a, DK570

9) Answer: C
Topic: Direct Quotes
References: LB43a, LH54, SFW40a, SFH38a, WH57d, NCH51d, DK570

10) Answer: A
Topic: Direct Quotes
References: LB43a, LH54, SFW40a, SFH38a, WH57c, NCH51a, DK570

11) Answer: B
Topic: Quotation Marks
References: LB43b, LH54, SFW40a, SFH38a, WH57e, NCH51c, DK570

12) Answer: A
Topic: Direct Quotes
References: LB43a, LH54, SFW40a, SFH38a, WH57e, NCH51e, DK570

13) Answer: A
Topic: Direct Quotes/Titles
References: LB43c, LH54d, SFW40a, SFH38a, WH57c, NCH51a, DK572

14) Answer: B
Topic: Direct Quotes
References: LB43a, LH54, SFW40a, SFH, SFH38a, WH57c, NCH51a, DK570

EXERCISE U: Using Other Punctuation Marks

1) Answer: B
Topic: Parentheses
References: LB44b, LH52b, SFW41a, SFH39a, WH58a, NCH52a, DK556

2) Answer: C
Topic: Colon
References: LB41, LH56a, SFW39b, SFH37b, WH54b, NCH49a, DK554

3) Answer: A
Topic: Brackets
References: LB44d, LH56b, SFW41b, SFH39b, WH58b, NCH52h, DK560

4) Answer: B
Topic: Parentheses
References: LB44b, LH56a, SFW41a, SFH39a, WH58a, NCH52a, DK556

5) Answer: A
Topic: Emphatic dash
References: LB44a, LH56c, SFW42a, SFH40a, WH58c, NCH52f, DK558

6) Answer: B
Topic: Slash
References: LB44e, LH56e, SFW42d, SFH40d, WH58e, NCH52o, DK564

217

7) Answer: A
Topic: Emphatic dash
References: LB44a, LH56c, SFW42a, SFH40a, WH58c, NCH52e, DK558

8) Answer: A
Topic: Emphatic dash
References: LB44a, LH56c, SFW42a, SFH40a, WH58c, NCH52e, DK558

9) Answer: C
Topic: Colon
References: LB41, LH52b, SFW39b, SFH37b, WH54b, NCH49a, DK554

10) Answer: B
Topic: Emphatic dash
References: LB44a, LH56c, SFW42a, SFH40a, WH58c, NCH52e, DK558

11) Answer: B
Topic: Emphatic dash
References: LB44a, LH56c, SFW42a, SFH40a, WH58c, NCH52e, DK558

12) Answer: A
Topic: Colon
References: LB41, LH52b, SFW39b, SFH37b, WH54b, NCH49a, DK554

13) Answer: C
Topic: Emphatic dash
References: LB44a, LH56c, SFW42a, SFH40a, WH58c, NCH52f, DK558

14) Answer: C
Topic: Brackets
References: LB44d, LH56b, SFW41b, SFH39b, WH58b, NCH52h, DK560

EXERCISE V: Using Capitalization and Italics

1) Answer: B
Topic: Capitalization
References: LB47, LH57, SFW43b, SFH41b, WH59b, NCH53b, DK588

2) Answer: B
Topic: Capitalization
References: LB47, LH57, SFW43b, SFH41b, WH59b, NCH53b, DK588

3) Answer: D
Topic: Capitalization
References: LB47, LH57, SFW43b, SFH41b, WH59b, NCH53a–c, DK588

4) Answer: C
Topic: Capitalization
References: LB47, LH57, SFW43b, SFH41b, WH59b, NCH53b, DK588

5) Answer: C
Topic: Italics
References: LB48, LH58, SFW43a, SFH41a, WH59b, NCH53b, DK585

6) Answer: D
Topic: Capitalization
References: LB47, LH57, SFW43b, SFH41b, WH59b, NCH53b, DK588

7) Answer: A
Topic: Italics
References: LB48, LH58, SFW43a, SFH41a, WH61b, NCH53b, DK585

8) Answer: C
Topic: Capitalization
References: LB47, LH57, SFW43b, SFH41b, WH59b, NCH53b, DK588

9) Answer: C
Topic: Italics
References: LB48, LH58, SFW43a, SFH41a, WH61b, NCH53e, DK585

10) Answer: B
Topic: Capitalization
References: LB47, LH57, SFW43b, SFH41b, WH59b, NCH53b, DK588

11) Answer: B
Topic: Capitalization
References: LB47, LH57, SFW43b, SFH41b, WH59b, NCH53b, DK588

12) Answer: D
Topic: Capitalization
References: LB47, LH57, SFW43b, SFH41b, WH59b, NCH53a–c, DK588

13) Answer: B
Topic: Capitalization
References: LB47, LH57, SFW43b, SFH41b, WH59b, NCH53b, DK588

14) Answer: A
Topic: Capitalization
References: LB47, LH57, SFW43b, SFH41b, WH59b, NCH53b, DK588

EXERCISE W: Using Abbreviation and Numbers

1) Answer: A
Topic: Abbreviations
References: LB49, LH61, SFW44b, SFH42a, WH60b, NCH54a, DK590

2) Answer: C
Topic: Numbers
References: LB50, LH60, SFW44c, SFH42b, WH63b, NCH54f, DK592

3) Answer: B
Topic: Numbers
References: LB50, LH60, SFW44c, SFH42b, WH63a, NCH54g, DK592

4) Answer: C
Topic: Numbers
References: LB50, LH60, SFW44c, SFH42b, WH63b, NCH54f, DK592

5) Answer: B
Topic: Numbers
References: LB50, LH60, SFW44c, SFH42b, WH63a, NCH54g, DK592

6) Answer: B
Topic: Numbers
References: LB50, LH60, SFW44c, SFH42b, WH63a, NCH54g, DK592

7) Answer: B
Topic: Abbreviations
References: LB49, LH61, SFW44b, SFH42a, WH60b, NCH54a, DK590

8) Answer: C
Topic: Abbreviations
References: LB49, LH61, SFW44b, SFH42a, WH60b, NCH54a, DK590

9) Answer: B
Topic: Abbreviations
References: LB49, LH61, SFW44b, SFH42a, WH60b, NCH54a, DK590

10) Answer: B
Topic: Abbreviations
References: LB49, LH61, SFW44b, SFH42a, WH60a, NCH54a, DK590

11) Answer: B
Topic: Numbers
References: LB50, LH60, SFW44c, SFH42b, WH63a, NCH54g, DK592

12) Answer: A
Topic: Numbers and abbreviations
References: LB49&50, LH61&61, SFW44b&c, SFH42a–b, WH63a, NCH54g, DK590, 592

13) Answer: C
Topic: Numbers
References: LB50, LH60, SFW44c, SFH42b, WH63a, NCH54g, DK592

14) Answer: B
Topic: Abbreviations
References: LB49, LH61, SFW44b, SFH42a, WH60b, NCH54a, DK590

15) Answer: A
Topic: Numbers
References: LB50, LH60, SFW44c, SFH42b, WH63a, NCH54i, DK592

EXERCISE X: Using Hyphens

1) Answer: A
Topic: Compound Words
References: LB46, LH59, SFW42c, SFH40c, WH62b, NCH55a, DK562

2) Answer: B
Topic: End of Line
References: LB46, LH59, SFW42c, SFH40c, WH62a, NCH55e, DK562

3) Answer: A
Topic: Compound Words
References: LB46, LH59, SFW42c, SFH40c, WH62b, NCH55a, DK562

4) Answer: B
Topic: End of Line
References: LB46, LH59, SFW42c, SFH40c, WH62a, NCH55e, DK562

5) Answer: B
Topic: Compound Words
References: LB46, LH59, SFW42c, SFH40c, WH62b, NCH55a, DK562

6) Answer: B
Topic: Compound Words
References: LB46, LH59, SFW42c, SFH40c, WH62b, NCH55a, DK562

7) Answer: A
Topic: Compound Words
References: LB46, LH59, SFW42c, SFH40c, WH62b, NCH55a, DK562

8) Answer: C
Topic: Compound Words
References: LB46, LH59, SFW42c, SFH40c, WH62b, NCH55a, DK562

9) Answer: A
Topic: Prefix, Suffix
References: LB46, LH59, SFW42c, SFH40c, WH62b, NCH55a, DK562

10) Answer: B
Topic: Compound Words
References: LB46, LH59, SFW42c, SFH40c, WH62b, NCH55a, DK562

11) Answer: B
Topic: Compound Words
References: LB46, LH59, SFW42c, SFH40c, WH62b, NCH55a, DK562

12) Answer: C
Topic: Compound Words
References: LB46, LH59, SFW42c, SFH40c, WH62b, NCH55a, DK562

13) Answer: A
Topic: Compound Words
References: LB46, LH59, SFW42c, SFH40c, WH62b, NCH55c, DK562

14) Answer: C
Topic: Prefix, Suffix
References: LB46, LH59, SFW42c, SFH40c, WH62b, NCH55a–c, DK562

15) Answer: C
Topic: Compound Words
References: LB46, LH59, SFW42c, SFH40c, WH62b, NCH55a, DK562